LEADING ACROSS THE ARC OF TIME

LEADING ACROSS THE ARC OF TIME

Commitment and Change in Higher Education

MARK L. PUTNAM

JOHNS HOPKINS UNIVERSITY PRESS

Baltimore

© 2025 Johns Hopkins University Press
All rights reserved. Published 2025
Printed in the United States of America on acid-free paper
2 4 6 8 9 7 5 3 1

Johns Hopkins University Press
2715 North Charles Street
Baltimore, Maryland 21218
www.press.jhu.edu

Library of Congress Cataloging-in-Publication Data

Names: Putnam, Mark L., 1960– author.
Title: Leading across the arc of time : commitment and
change in higher education / Mark L. Putnam.
Description: Baltimore : Johns Hopkins University Press, 2025. |
Includes bibliographical references and index.
Identifiers: LCCN 2024021287 | ISBN 9781421450735 (hardcover) |
ISBN 9781421450742 (ebook)
Subjects: LCSH: Universities and colleges—United States—Administration. |
Education, Higher—Aims and objectives—United States. |
Educational change—United States.
Classification: LCC LB2341 .P88 2025 | DDC 378.1/
010973—dc23/eng/20241009
LC record available at https://lccn.loc.gov/2024021287

A catalog record for this book is available from the British Library.

*Special discounts are available for bulk purchases of this book. For more information,
please contact Special Sales at specialsales@jh.edu.*

For Tammy

CONTENTS

PREFACE

During the summer of 2023, I received a text message from a college president I have known for many years—a successful and seasoned leader. He was seeking a conversation to hear my impressions on the prospects for higher education, particularly among independent colleges in the Midwest. The final words of this text were, "I don't think our board really believes me."

This book is for him and many others like him—administrators, trustees, faculty members, and policymakers—who are working hard to preserve institutions during a time of immense societal change, institutional stress, and uncertainty. The challenge is that many stakeholders associated with colleges and universities participate in an enterprise well known for its ambiguity. Constituents do not all share the same sense of purpose or utilize the same measures for success. The lack of shared understanding regarding the history that informs the present and drives the future weakens our capacity for an effective response. Some cling to patterns of the past. Many carry perspectives informed by personal experiences in higher education long out of date or highly contextual to a specific time and place. Suffering under the weight of shifting expectations, the pressure is to react rather than respond. The feeling of risk that a program, service, or activity—even an entire institution—may be lost is an enormous weight to bear and is fraught with conflict.

Across the long arc of time, the postsecondary universe has changed immensely, but not in the way many stakeholders would prefer. Change occurs through assimilation over long periods of time, which is both a strength and a weakness. Its strength is found in the reassurance of reliability and durability; its weakness is found in a slavishness to conformity and conventional wisdom. The paradox of higher education is that innovation and compliance are joined at the hip. Through time, new ideas, which lead to novel practices, eventually become rigid patterns leading to hardened expectations adopted by myriad organizations and associations comprising the vast postsecondary universe. Change in the college and university context is responsive to many competing interests in society but is governed by an invisible hand collectively manipulated over long periods of time.

An example of this pattern of change is found in the years after the release of the Truman Commission Report, issued in 1947 with the title *Higher Education for American Democracy* (President's Commission 1947). Though this was a government report issued by the President's Commission on Higher Education, which was appointed by President Harry S. Truman, the benefit was not in its political power but in its timely expression of a set of imperatives. The report became a stimulant for action by outlining the needs of the postwar nation with great clarity, and then setting a proposed agenda for the national higher education enterprise to consider. This process ushered in a period of extended assimilation lasting at least 30 years, despite the confining structures inherent in the postsecondary universe at the time the report was released. Today's critics of higher education issue the indictment that the patterns of organization now well-formed since the 1940s, and once viewed as innovations, are holding the enterprise back. They advocate for interventions that will change higher education as we know it. Those working in colleges and universities have seen this recurring process many times before. The pathway of assimilation is inherently gradual, and the formation of conformities reliably predictable, to the impatient frustration of many.

This book seeks to elevate the discourse. The higher education landscape is littered with strategic and tactical advice put forth in the absence of an understanding of how the change process works in this context. The first four chapters of this book are presented in part 1, *The Sound of Inevitability*. These chapters lay the foundation for understanding how the change process in higher education emerges by exploring the unfolding of history and the development of organizational theory. The first chapter, *When Time Is on Our Side*, does this on a conceptual level, offering a set of organizational metaphors helpful in thinking about how the cyclical process of managing change through assimilation eventually hardens into patterns of conformity and convention. Effective leadership in this context is further explored as an acknowledgment of this pattern is essential to an accurate assessment of the change challenge at hand. Chapter 2, *There's a Reason for This*, explores the historical context in which colleges and universities formed and evolved to reinforce a pattern of conformity at both the institutional and national levels. The third chapter, *Why Can't I Escape?*, delves into the organizational dynamics consistently manifested in the management of colleges and universities. Well-established organizational theory in higher education, practically applied to the present condition, is an aid to interpreting the patterns of change typical in institutions of higher education. Chapter 4, *The Six-Pack of Change*, applies the conceptual framework and the historical context to six categories of change that have been consistently referenced as the primary areas of interest in change management for postsecondary education since the early 1980s.

Chapters 5–7 are presented in part 2, *We Learn Big Things a Little at a Time*. These chapters apply the recursive process of gradual change to organizational governance and management. Chapter 5, *The Presidency Is Not a Person*, presses against the notion that advancing an institution rests upon a single individual. While the president is a person, the presidency is an office, supported by a range of individuals. Chapter 6, *A Community of Trust*, focuses on the role of the governing board, which is an institution within an institution, and is most closely associated with leading across the arc of time. This is as much a relational task as it is an organizational task, since the trust invested in the board is collectively held by all the members. Chapter 7, *We're in This Together*, addresses the interaction of governance and management, and the important role the faculty plays in guiding the development of the educational experience. Taken together these three chapters look comprehensively at the interplay of shared governance involving the governing board, the faculty (in its role as a governing body), and the presidency. All have defined roles in governance, while the presidency has the concurrent responsibility for management. The responsibilities are invariably shared yet diffused across an institution in which organizational history and culture play a considerable role.

Part 3, *The Illusion of Control*, presents chapters 8 through 10. The decisions and actions of various individuals, groups, and entities external to our institutions do more to shape the higher education enterprise than most realize. Chapter 8, *Who Is the*

Learner and What Should They Learn? focuses on students and the teaching and learning process. Education is a fundamentally human enterprise in which the teacher and the learner are in a complex intellectual relationship. What students should learn is the subject of endless debate as their expressed needs and interests are contrasted with the expectations of academic disciplines, professional fields of study, and society in general. Chapter 9, *My Hands Are Tied*, explores the complexity of the legal, regulatory, and policy frameworks that both enable and constrain the process of assimilation. These frameworks are also the most potent force of conformity in the postsecondary universe. Chapter 10, *Time Will Tell*, takes a look at the future and explores the marketplace for higher education, the dynamics of change, the limited degrees of freedom available, and the need for a fresh national conversation. Understanding and accepting what is in the span of control, and is actionable within a reasonable framework of decision-making, is the foundation for setting an agenda for change.

While this book will be of interest to those who think about higher education, it is intended for those working in higher education. Consultants, journalists, and pundits have something important to offer through aggregate observations of national trends, but these colleagues are unreliable predictors of the future. Practitioners actively serving in colleges and universities are better positioned to see and interpret the recursive patterns of incremental innovation and conformity that facilitate change through the arc of time. When they understand and interpret their own institutional histories set against the backdrop of national history, they empower themselves and others to embrace assimilation as the process most likely to lead to sustained success in the years to come.

ACKNOWLEDGMENTS

Writing brings to mind the personal and professional relationships of a lifetime. Colleagues and mentors too numerous to count have been my thought and conversation partners through the decades. I owe so many a deep debt of gratitude. Of note is Robert Zemsky, who served as my executive coach for nearly 20 years. For long periods of my career, we spoke almost weekly as he tracked my progress, offered insights, expressed words of caution, and joined me in celebration. As noted in the text of chapter 5, the three college and university presidents I served with over a period of 17 years—Claire Gaudiani, Richard Freeland, and Joseph Aoun—remain with me today as voices echoing with the lessons of the past and the possibilities of the future. Sharon McDade, my dissertation advisor, set me on the path of exploring the literature I rely on throughout this book and encouraged my early attempts at teaching, writing, and leadership.

In more recent years, I have benefited immensely from the counsel and advice of the three board chairs I have served with at Central College thus far in my tenure—Dave Wesselink, Lanny Little, and Tej Dhawan. I refer to them as the "Oracle of the Three

Chairs" and press them into service together from time to time for shared deliberations on a matter before me.

Two friends who have spent many hours in conversation with me exploring the ideas I present in this book are John Schmidt and Eric Sickler. They have been helpful sounding boards for ideas through the years.

I work with an amazing set of colleagues who serve on the Senior Leadership Team at Central College, and I am deeply grateful to them for their partnership and patience, and for teaching me so much. In particular, Sunny Eighmy and Carma Sturtz made it possible for me to write this book. Sunny's superb editing skills were applied to the manuscript. Carma organized my work and managed my schedule to allow me time to write. Both have been a great source of encouragement along the way and have my deepest gratitude.

Throughout this project, my immediate audience has been the Board of Trustees of Central College. We have forged an effective partnership marked by mutual trust and respect. In many ways this book is a compendium of conversations we have had through the years. I am indebted to this board for having patience with our shared learning experience, modeling the practices of disciplined governance, and always remaining unfailingly cordial.

My family is the source of immense joy. My wife, Tammy, is the center of my universe. Our daughter, Emma, and her husband, Carr; our daughter, Greta, and her husband, Jason; along with our grandchildren, Christopher, Cece, and Eliza, inspire me to be the best person I can be every day. I love you all.

PART I

The Sound of Inevitability

It seems higher education has been on the brink of disaster since the University of Bologna was founded in 1088. This is at least the historical narrative presented to us. In one sense this is true. Whatever form it has taken, in whatever part of the world identified, and through whatever time period one wishes to define, the enterprise has at times struggled.

In another sense this is not true based on the lived experience of institutions across the long arc of time. Enduring periods of plenty and scarcity, amidst societal turmoil and calm, and with an ever-expanding body of knowledge, higher education has coped with change by reinterpreting and readapting. It's not always an orderly affair. Controversies abound and conflict arises as the demand for change is declared. The process by which change occurs, however, is recursive, incremental, and episodic.

Still, the need for human learning persists and the response seeks to accommodate the emerging need. It is not always timely, and sometimes it misses the mark. Yet we work with what we have, as imperfect as it may be in the moment. In time, the innovating and conserving energies of the academic community lead to evolving change. Through all this history there remains one important reality: we are still here.

CHAPTER 1

When Time Is on Our Side

"I've decided we are going to have the 'Decade of the Arts' over the next five years." I heard this statement uttered by a college president in a meeting held during the late 1990s. Remarkably, no one in the room laughed out loud, but sideward glances and restrained smiles were evident among the participants. No such initiative ever emerged. The vision was compelling. The time frame was a death knell.

Time is the greatest asset available to colleges and universities, but it is also the most misplayed. In the moment, time feels like an immediate constraint, lorded over by the tyranny of the urgent. In this context, time feels stingy. The arc of time is different. There, time is a gradually unfolding process through which the most important things are achieved. It is generous when used wisely. The example above inverted these two characteristics of time by attempting to constrain a grand ambition for the arts to a narrowly defined, limited, and timebound project. An imaginative future was betrayed by an unrealistic time horizon.

Misunderstandings of time do not end there. Looking back through time can also lead to distorted thinking. The tendency is to compress time when reinterpreting the events of history. Leaders fall prey to a misperception of the time it takes to do great things in the present day. Most everything seen before us today took longer to develop than one might think. Several years ago, my institution announced the awarding of a multimillion-dollar grant from a family foundation for a capital project. A few days later I was in a casual conversation with a member of the college community who congratulated me on the gift and then asked, "Were you surprised?" I was taken aback by the question but realized not everyone is acquainted with the work involved in obtaining such a grant. I explained the effort required about 18 months and involved many steps. What I did not share was that the current members of the family had been engaged with the college over the previous 25 years, and the college received its first gift from a member of the family nearly a century ago. Many of the most profound achievements colleges and universities have produced have only been possible through a long arc of time involving multiple generations.

For an enterprise that dates back centuries in this country, time should be viewed as a critical asset. Instead, societal accelerants have pressed colleges and universities to process change too quickly, or at least attempt to do so. Yet the arc of time in the postsecondary universe is largely unresponsive to the demands presented to it. Observers view this as recalcitrance. Blame abounds and is pointed in many directions.

In one sense, higher education is changing all the time. In another sense, it never changes. To some extent both assertions are true. The subtlety is that higher education does change. It changes through a process of gradual assimilation, which invariably leads to conformity, eventually resulting in rigid convention. This pattern has a long history. I rely on three themes, represented by three seemingly unrelated organizational images, to understand and interpret how this works. The first two illustrate how change is facilitated or inhibited in the postsecondary context. The third provides some clues about how to manage in such a landscape. The combination of these disparate images is a bit of a hodgepodge, but then so is higher education.

Cathedrals and Spaceships

Two dimensions help describe the role time plays in understanding the capacity for change in higher education. These apply at the institutional level as well as the more systemic levels of the national enterprise. The first, represented by the image of a cathedral, helps in understanding that some of the core characteristics of colleges and universities are timeless and difficult, if not impossible, to change. The second reflects how change really happens in a timebound reality, which is through a process of assimilation. For this I borrow an example from science fiction that illustrates how the passage of time is a natural filtration process that in the end separates fleeting changes from those that will last.

Construction of the Cathedral of St. John the Divine began December 27, 1892. It is today about two-thirds of the way to completion. I remember visiting the Episcopal cathedral located on the upper west side of Manhattan nearly 40 years ago. The group tour included a stop by the carving shed where masons and carvers—truly artisans—were shaping stonework and sculptures to be set in place piece by piece. Our guide, through her description of the work, helped me realize the obvious. Highly skilled workers, many beginning as apprentices, would spend significant portions of their lives on this task. They were not there at the beginning, nor would they ever see the end of the project despite many years of service.

That image has stayed with me ever since. The work is dedicated to something that goes beyond the interests of any single person or any narrowly defined span of time. It is an intergenerational task of stewardship that cares more about an enduring legacy than a momentary achievement. It's enough to simply have a meaningful role that contributes to a grand and inspiring vision. Such notions seem lost today.

The image of a cathedral represents what I have valued about my career in higher education. Institutions of higher learning, like cathedrals, never seem to be finished. They are always a work in progress. More importantly, they are intergenerational. The dependency of one generation on another is structurally based, just as one stone is layered upon another. It takes a long time to craft each stone or ornament, and once set in place seems practically impossible to move. Likewise, long-established patterns and traditions in a college or university seem immovable. Sometimes that may be true. Yet the stewardship of an inheritance into a legacy involves anticipation and preparation for change that is inevitable as society asks new questions and pursues novel answers. Cathedrals have a capacity to adapt across centuries, albeit slowly and subtly.

Trustees, faculty, and administrators, who play key roles through extended years on campuses, are increasingly pressed to shorten the time horizon of thinking. This is a perilous choice. Colleges and universities, buttressed by layer upon layer of internal and external regulations, conventions, and traditions, are incorrigible in resisting change. The rigid systems that undergird institutions are like a complex of cathedrals nested together with many interconnecting touch points. The complicated network of federal and state laws and regulations, accreditation policies, and standards of professional practice define and inform institutional work. Together, they bind universities in a maze of interdependent patterns of predictable activity.

I often hear of the crying need for higher education to change its undergirding educational and organizational model. For me, this sounds like the unworthy task of disassembling a cathedral, moving it across the street, and reassembling it. In view of this, some have argued that such a systemic change process is far too difficult to undertake, and it would be easier to simply start over. Fair enough. Yet the systems into which this new nimbler enterprise would be built are the very same. Successful change requires a gradual reset in structural limitations rather than an attempt to supplant them entirely. There are obvious virtues to the enduring strength of institutions that last centuries, but the facility for rapid change is not among them. As vocal critics of higher education scream for enterprise-wide change, the enterprise yawns.

However, change still occurs, though not at the pace many prefer. Adorning the entrance to Jordan Hall, the oldest structure remaining on my campus built in 1905, is a sign etched in stone that reads: "Natural Sciences." That building now houses programs in the humanities and social sciences. It's a daily reminder for me that the assumptions of one generation may not be those of the next. Old intents remain visible even as the structures of the past are repurposed in service of the future. Change emerges across the arc of time.

Leaving behind a medieval image, I move to science fiction to illustrate another dimension of the change challenge for colleges and universities. I have been a *Star Trek* fan for many years, though admittedly, I lapsed a bit with the many spin-offs that have extended the saga through time. The various starships and crew members through the evolving story have encountered an alien collective known as the Borg. The Borg is best understood as a hive of living humanoid drones linked together as cybernetic organisms through advanced biotechnology. Not being a species that naturally procreates, the Borg grows the collective through conquest and capture. Those captured are forcibly overtaken and injected with nanoprobes that link to installed anatomical appliances. The result is the elimination of individual thought and action. The collective defines reality.

Moving through space in a giant futuristic cube-like spaceship, the Borg will approach a target ship, hail the competing captain, and, in a machine-like chorus of voices, announce the following:

> We are the Borg. Lower your shields and surrender your ship. We will add your biological and technological distinctiveness to our own. Your culture will adapt to serve us. Resistance is futile. You will be assimilated.

Higher education is the Borg. Generation after generation there have been attempts by well-meaning explorers to create completely new models of postsecondary education to supplant the existing order. Leaders are told that some new initiative will change higher education "as we know it." As soon as this statement is uttered, a large dark cube appears over the horizon of space, with centuries of conformity and compliance contained within. The explorers travel through the postsecondary universe promoting their next disruptive change until the collective voice rings out from the giant cube saying, "We are the higher education establishment. Resistance is futile. You will be assimilated."

The ensuing pattern is familiar. Entities created to disrupt the known order are designed, built, and launched. Pundits who write articles and speak at conferences say historical institutions are under threat of extinction. The rhetoric becomes frenetic with predictions of imminent demise. It's not that the proposed innovations are without merit or consequence. The problem is the hyperbole ignores a simple reality—the structures and systems of higher education are unyielding. The great expanse of the postsecondary universe emerged without design. It has no leadership. It has no center. It has no clearly defined shape. It is not in the control of any single individual or entity. It is a collective with a breathtaking capacity for assimilation.

Taken together, these images help us explain two concurrent and yet contradictory propositions about the character of higher education. The structural elements that make the national higher education enterprise seem sturdy and timeless, like a cathedral, are widely embraced by convention. Then as new ideas are introduced, they are gradually assimilated through an interactive and recursive process, like the Borg. Through time, the differences between tradition and innovation are reconciled by the collective. New ideas are filtered and sorted, gradually leading the academy back to a pattern of conformity, which eventually becomes rigid convention. Rinse and repeat.

Some of the largest stones in a cathedral are those not seen. They are the stones that form the foundation and bear the weight of the entire structure. Observers tend not to think about them as eyes are drawn to the more decorative elements in the design, but without them the structure cannot stand. It is possible to renew or replace the peripheral or ornamental elements of the building; to replace a foundational element is another matter entirely.

The largest and heaviest stone in the educational cathedral is represented in the following statement: *Education is fundamentally a human enterprise.* This concept is reflected throughout human history. People learn from each other. They benefit from the knowledge, skill, and experience of those who have gone before them. Learners respect teachers and the expertise they have to share. Learning is at its core relational, and the younger the learner, the more important that relationship becomes. Yet the desire for a teacher seems to always remain with a learner, regardless of age. Whatever else may change in higher education, this foundation stone will not move—but that has not stopped many from trying.

Educating humans is messy. The earliest stages of life present learners as essentially dependent. Parents are the first teachers. As the journey extends through time, the task of education is to enable the student to become a more independent learner. Though there are individual differences that affect the process and outcomes, the natural course of human development informs and is informed by education. Teachers play an evolving role in this process. Independent learners, however, do not typically express a desire or intent to be separated from the benefits of a teacher. It's simply that they are less dependent on them as the acquisition of knowledge, coupled with maturity, naturally enables more independence. Lifelong learning is the acknowledgment that even through adult life, there are times when a learner becomes a teacher and a teacher becomes a learner. Education remains a fundamentally human enterprise of interactive learning.

Another stone, less hefty and more recently set in place, is one described as education for democracy, education for citizenship, or education as a public good. Though the phrasing varies, the underlying sentiment is the same: *Education benefits everyone.* The expansion of education through the 20th century is an impressive tale of its own. Compulsory primary and secondary education formed the foundation that would eventually lead to a societal expectation for tertiary education as a broad-based opportunity. The problem is that educating humans is expensive.

These twin foundation stones reinforce a societal ambition for education to be inherently relational and broadly available. The incompatibility is that policymakers want this to take less time and less money. There are virtues in pursuing initiatives that will make learning more efficient and more effective. The unbridled enthusiasm of the innovators pursuing productivity, however, often conflicts with long-established societal values foundational to education. This point of friction is where the assimilation process is triggered. Enter the Borg. Policymakers, eager to reduce time and cost, partner with innovators eager to make a profit. Once this becomes visible to the higher education enterprise, the assimilation process begins, and resistance is futile.

An example of how assimilation works is found in the iterative process witnessed in recent decades as information technology enabled technology-based course design. The efficacy of these technologies was self-evident from the beginning. It was easy to anticipate the inevitability of change far in advance. The miscalculation, however, was that technology companies believed they could supplant the higher education establishment through rapid disruptive change and turn a profit. Policymakers believed they could reduce cost. What the printing press, radio, television, video recording, computerization, videoconferencing, and livestreaming could not accomplish during past technological change cycles would finally be achieved as technology would now redefine higher education. The plan never had any hope for success. The assimilation process is an irresistible force, and a foundation stone is an immovable object. Technology companies, supported by venture capital, initially presented an online model of education intended to be infinitely scalable, asynchronous, and adaptive. The system would be built by technology experts, relying on content experts. It was envisioned to turn a healthy profit given its incredible efficiency. Policymakers salivated. Then it didn't work. The relational aspects of learning were left out.

The ensuing assimilation process undertaken by the higher education enterprise restored the human element by dramatically limiting the scale of cohorts and engaging instructors to lead individual courses. They were aided and abetted by accrediting associations, federal and state agencies, and professional societies that gradually aligned around best practices. Individual institutions and state systems began to develop the technology infrastructure and professional competencies required to enter the marketplace. Many did so through contract services with outside vendors, including some of the same companies plotting the original overthrow. While new revenues were available, institutional costs increased, and existing students then enrolled in online courses to replace or supplement their on-campus study. Instructional patterns changed as the demand for flexibility increased, leading to hybrid, hy-flex, and low residency programs of study. In the end, policymakers were presented with increased costs and the technology companies realized little, if any, profits in a business model now retreating into a service industry to support the existing higher education community. The assimilation process has been impressive to watch, and it will continue to unfold for years to come. These things take time, and the fullness of the impacts has not yet been measured.

The changes already adopted by institutions are significant as learning technologies continue to reshape pedagogical design. The ways in which public and private not-for-profit institutions do business has been profoundly affected by the original for-profit experiments. But the futility of resistance to the overwhelming force of the national higher education enterprise, coupled with the remarkable capacity this enormous enterprise has for assimilation, is on full display as the giant cube quietly passes through the debris field, collecting what it will.

These two metaphors, one historical and one futuristic, provide a reminder that higher education, like cathedrals and intergalactic space cubes, is huge. The cathedral illustrates that colleges and universities come with an intended sense of permanence as institutions, and they are designed and built to reflect this quality. That is not to suggest such places are invulnerable. I once wandered past a former Catholic church in Ireland with a sign in front of the building promoting the Black Dragon Kickboxing Gym. The loss of a single or even several institutions, however, does not undermine the premise that colleges and universities are intended to remain. Campuses, buildings, endowments, and tenure are all stones set in place, reinforced by the frameworks of laws, regulations, rules, and policies surrounding them. It provides a sense of place and permanence.

The Borg, as the collective moves through time and space, represents something different. It is the more dynamic aspect of our institutions, where information is actively acquired, and patterns are recognized and copied. This leads to the creation of standards, conventions, and norms that define accepted, even acceptable, practices. These patterns are hard to change once they become the expected behavioral pathways for colleges and universities. They gradually solidify as the narratives of best practice are rehearsed through institutional and professional associations. The adopted patterns are not immutable, they just change very slowly. Yet the aim of assimilation is about normalizing new patterns of behavior, promoting conformity, and stabilizing expectations. This makes the process recursive as small incremental changes are explored and adopted through an iterative process.

Both aspects result in reinforcing rigidities. Policies are often as hard to renovate as buildings. The key is understanding lasting change does not come to higher education from institutional reproduction, replacement, or revolution. It comes from assimilation that is almost undetectable in the moment but manifested through time as qualities of evolutionary change emerge. Seen through this lens, time is an asset, not a liability. It is an overwhelming pattern of gradual, inexorable change through assimilation. The question is whether to resist change, force change, or cooperate with change through the practices of relentless patience and relentless execution.

Lessons in Canal Building

Institutions of higher education are firmly grounded—their greatest source of enduring strength. They also are embedded in an enormous and highly complex enterprise that is competent in reestablishing equilibrium. This framework was not in anyone's design. It simply formed through time. I offer here another image intended to illustrate how institutions can work effectively in an environment characterized by these rigidities. The challenge of building a canal is a helpful place to begin.

In the 1880s, a flamboyant Frenchman, Ferdinand de Lesseps, had an enormous idea. He announced a plan to connect the Atlantic and Pacific Oceans by a sea-level canal through Panama. As a builder and developer, he had some degree of credibility since he had already completed a project for the construction of the Suez Canal in 1869. More importantly, he was a skilled and well-connected promoter, who spoke with great confidence. His personal style attracted wealth and influence. Through private investment he raised the funds needed to attempt this vast project. Despite his impressive ambition, the effort failed miserably, leaving corruption and scandal in his wake.

David McCullough, in his history of the Panama Canal, *The Path between the Seas*, described de Lesseps's experience as follows:

> The extraordinary venture had lasted more than a decade. It had cost, according to the best estimates, 1,435,000,000 francs—about $287,000,000—which was 1,000,000,000 francs more than the cost of the Suez Canal, far more in fact than had ever before been spent on any one peaceful undertaking of any kind. The number of lives lost, a subject that had been strangely avoided throughout the affair, had not been determined, nor was it ever to be with certainty.

He continued:

> It had indeed been a blunder on such an inordinate scale, a failure of such overwhelming magnitude, its shock waves extending to so very many levels, that nobody knew quite what to make of it; and as time passed, the inclination was to dismiss it as the folly of one man. (McCullough 1977, 235)

Many factors were involved in this debacle, but it is clear de Lesseps's rhetorical audacity far exceeded his organizational capacity.

In the end, the canal was completed by a clear-eyed understanding of the true challenges presented, which were addressed through the thoughtful application of carefully designed interventions, learned through collective wisdom and experience. The first issue to be confronted was the scourge of malaria and yellow fever, which took the lives of as many as 22,000 in the earlier failed attempt. It was the study of disease and the discovery of mosquito-borne illness by scientists that paved the way for surviving the tropical environment. Second, it was the shared realization that the fundamental engineering challenge was not to begin by building a canal but instead a railroad system that would make the construction of a canal feasible by moving personnel and equipment across the landscape. Third, the development of a vast infrastructure of support systems was essential to sustaining the workforce. Entire local communities were built to care for the well-being of the workers for many years. Finally, it was acknowledged that a sea-level waterway was simply not possible to design. Locks were constructed to lift and lower ships through terrain that could only be mastered through technology.

Eventually, it would not be the blind ambition of an individual but the will of a nation, the United States of America, animated by the expertise and effort of many, that would build the Panama Canal. "From the time the first public declaration regarding an intent to build a canal connecting the Atlantic and Pacific Oceans was presented by de Lesseps in 1875, to the opening of the Panama Canal in 1914, nearly four decades had passed. The Panama Canal and the Suez Canal share only one thing in common—they can both be described according to the standard dictionary definition as canals. That is where the comparison ends" (Putnam 2011).

The construction of the Panama Canal provides many lessons. The characteristics of Ferdinand de Lesseps's missteps are the same ones seen in higher education in recent decades. He was a showman displaying great rhetorical flair. This had the benefit of attracting financial support for the endeavor but also the detriment of allowing his ambition to cloud the reality of the challenge at hand. This kind of daring self-confidence is sometimes on display among higher education's leaders, with statements that ignore the reality of the ambition presented by papering over the true nature of the task. It is possible de Lesseps might have found sufficient support for his idea had he built on the momentum he gained in completing the Suez Canal, but he redefined the anticipated project in Panama as a larger and far more complex task given the profound differences in terrain. Some could argue that he was just a charlatan. I tend to think of him more as a visionary divorced from reality. Rhetorical flair has its place in animating action, but such action must be sustained through long arcs of time when the challenges mount, unexpected distractions emerge, and people are weary. Managing expectations and doing the hard work of careful planning, focused resource allocation, disciplined implementation, and timely adaptations are core responsibilities of institutional leaders. This requires sustained effort through time.

Institutional leaders are too often guilty of the same types of assertions, though on a far less ambitious scale. I continue to see those in the higher education enterprise who understate the reality of the presenting circumstances and offer glossy plans without completing the necessary due diligence with rigorous research and analysis. One day a colleague said to me in frustration, "I am swimming in data, but have no information with which I can make a decision." It was a telling comment that rang true with authenticity but reflected an unfortunate reality.

The building of the Panama Canal required a multilayered and multiphased approach that could only be successful with the consistent and well-informed investment of time, energy, and money over an extended period of years. The patience required to first create the conditions in which a canal could be built was the single most important ingredient in the eventual success. Some institutional leaders today tend to be more like de Lesseps and just start digging a canal. The incredible infrastructure demanded, however, meant there would be a long delay in beginning work on anything one might describe as a canal.

For institutions, the same is true. The antecedents to long-term success are too often ignored. There are times when a curricular innovation requires a reformulation of academic policies to create the conditions necessary for successful design and implementation. Motivating donor support can take considerable time to cultivate and secure through multiyear pledges. Moving through related regulatory and accreditation processes can be arduous, but it is essential to creating a viable program. Innovations also can create collateral and cascading effects that need to be taken into consideration. The list goes on. These are the tasks of management, supported by governance, considered to be normative. Yet the urgent press of the current conditions, both internal and external to institutions, is yielding incentives to accelerate change irresponsibly. The result is a growing pattern of rapid attempts to intervene quickly, without regard for the need for interpretive and adaptive planning in a highly volatile context. The endless search for low-hanging fruit is a form of conventional wisdom, but at some point a ladder is needed to go after the fruit that is hard to reach.

Institutional work is highly contextual and nuanced, but the tendency is to copy success or, as some describe it, "R&D"—that is, "Rip-off & Duplicate." This is the Suez/Panama inversion. Benchmarking has its uses, but slavishness to comparison yields the contradiction of seeking to pursue distinctiveness by means of following others. Too often leaders look like six-year-olds playing soccer, gathered in a clump and chasing the ball around the field. Conformity is the shadow side of assimilation. It leads to the formation of conventional wisdom. The resulting trap confines the expectations of others as a safe harbor from critics, but it concedes the opportunity to attempt a novel approach.

Those engaged in the leadership of postsecondary institutions are facing considerable challenges. There is an understandable sense of urgency, but it is essential to see the present reality in a larger framework of interpretation. If driven solely by the next incoming class or the next fiscal year (while acknowledging the importance of those checkpoints), the areas of inquiry and analysis that will help us better define the steps that can lead us beyond the tyranny of the urgent are closed off.

When time is viewed as an asset, not a liability, the conversation changes. Sometimes accepting a less-than-perfect present creates space necessary to design a better future. When institutional leaders adopt a posture of patience, create the space needed for calm consideration, and respond rather than react, more solution-thinking that is clear-eyed and realistic can be inspired. The alternatives of audacity and austerity rarely produce a satisfactory result. The best thinking is revealed when authenticity is pursued. The complex task of building a canal through unforgiving terrain is a useful image in thinking about leading a college or university through difficult days.

The chapters that follow build on these ideas and outline the origins of the present reality, the dynamics of leadership expressed through governance and management, and the demands of the future for which leaders are preparing. Along the way I will make use of the three organizational images I have explored. Leaders can gain a sense of awe and inspiration from cathedrals that remind institutions of the best and most important enduring qualities. Leaders must take seriously the overwhelming power of assimilation by which change is processed and normalized within the collective. Leaders must respect the task of building a canal in conditions that are intimidating but still possible to overcome with equal measures of humility and determination. Leading across the arc of time requires all three.

CHAPTER 2

There's a Reason for This

Near the end of the George W. Bush administration in 2007–8, I attended a series of meetings in Washington, DC, that related to the work product of the Commission on the Future of Higher Education, commonly called the Spellings Commission. It was so named because Margaret Spellings, the US Secretary of Education in those years, convened the panel. Its stated purpose, as outlined in its charter, was as follows:

> The purpose of the Commission is to consider how best to improve our system of higher education to ensure that our graduates are well prepared to meet our future workforce needs and are able to participate fully in the changing economy. To accomplish this purpose, the Commission shall consider federal, state, local, and institutional roles in higher education and analyze whether the current goals of higher education are appropriate and achievable. (Commission on the Future 2006, 30)

The ultimate report was titled *A Test of Leadership: Charting the Future of Higher Education* (2006).

Typical of government-sponsored meetings in Washington, I was sitting in a windowless hotel conference room. My involvement grew from my role as an executive committee member for the National Postsecondary Education Cooperative (NPEC, pronounced "en-peck").

NPEC was a voluntary partnership of postsecondary institutions, associations, government agencies, and organizations that received funding from the National Center for Education Statistics (NCES) in the US Department of Education. NPEC's mission was to promote the quality, comparability, and utility of postsecondary data and information that support policy development at the federal, state, and institution levels. In this setting, the assignment related to the ways in which the postsecondary data universe could support the imperatives set forth in the Spellings Commission report, namely, access, affordability, accountability, innovation, lifelong learning, and global competitiveness. The report concluded:

> In short, the commission believes it is imperative that the nation give urgent attention to improving its system of higher education.
>
> The future of our country's colleges and universities is threatened by global competitive pressures, powerful technological developments, restraints on public finance and serious structural limitations that cry out for reform.
>
> Our report has recommended strategic actions designed to make higher education more accessible, more affordable, and more accountable, while maintaining world-class quality. Our colleges and universities must become more transparent, faster to respond to rapidly changing circumstances and increasingly productive in order to deal effectively with the powerful forces of change they now face.

But reaching these goals will also require difficult decisions and major changes from many others beyond the higher education community.

The commission calls on policymakers to address the needs of higher education in order to maintain social mobility and a high standard of living. We call on the business community to become directly and fully engaged with government and higher education leaders in developing innovative structures for delivering 21st-century educational services—and in providing the necessary financial and human resources for that purpose.

Finally, we call on the American public to join in our commitment to improving the postsecondary institutions on which so much of our future—as individuals and as a nation—relies.

Working together, we can build on the past successes of U.S. higher education to create an improved and revitalized postsecondary system that is better tailored to the demands, as well as the opportunities, of a new century. (Commission on the Future 2006, 27)

Secretary Spellings addressed the members of NPEC to promote the need to share data, information, and analysis as they were essential to advancing the commission's presented interests. Yet as I sat in the room, I grew increasingly frustrated by the expectations being presented and the arrogance that accompanied them. These were the waning days of the Bush administration. Taking aim at a colossal change process with so little time left on the clock ignored the reality at hand. The hallway conversations affirmed my own impressions as eye rolling, accompanied by head shaking, were the general responses. To be fair, it is not that the recommendations lacked merit. But the notion there is even an organized "system" of higher education is misguided. I realized then the curse of every generation is the loss of memory. The reports and recommendations of commissions, committees, and task forces too often ignore the origins of the postsecondary universe seen today and what it takes to redesign a rigid, undefined structure built through generations. However, society persists in the attempt to "reform" higher education by government mandate, as if it can be simply willed to happen.

Sometimes I wonder if there is a standard recipe used by federal and state governments for this purpose. If so, it probably reads something like this:

1. Begin with sweeping generalizations sufficient to explain the perceived problems.
2. Oversimplify the circumstances to avoid complexity and ambiguity.
3. Reduce understanding to a small set of solutions for purposes of implementation.
4. Add a measure of false precision to be confident that a means-end reversal can be achieved.
5. Mix the above in a panel, commission, task force, or committee. Stir vigorously.
6. Present the one-size-fits-all results in a written report with tables and charts.
7. Garnish with an executive summary.
8. Serve at a press conference.

One wonders why leaders continue to repeat this recipe when the results are so unsatisfying. Some of the same core elements presented by the Spellings Commission were articulated during the early 1990s from the Clinton administration, called State Postsecondary Review Entities (SPREs) proposed through the US Department of Education. The idea intended to create the Program

Integrity Triad, relying on a coordinated structure involving the US Department of Education, state higher education agencies, and regional accreditors. At last, the government believed it would be able to hold colleges and universities accountable for outcomes—except it couldn't work and was eventually scrapped.

As I listened to Secretary Spellings, her emphasis was also on the theme of accountability. She made clear the Spellings Commission report was the natural extension of the administration's No Child Left Behind policy, which also was deeply rooted in accountability. For me this was just another process designed to change higher education, without any understanding of how change in this setting actually works. I began referring to the Spellings Commission work as the "Son of SPRE," confident, and yet disappointed, that it was unlikely to produce any results. Unfortunately, well-intended and thoughtful ideas are no match for diffused and dispersed systems like the one that has evolved. While it is not possible to fully define or map this system, it is possible to understand it conceptually. Like a cathedral, it was built through generations, one stone at a time.

The Origins of the "System"

In his book *A Perfect Mess: The Unlikely Ascendancy of American Higher Education* (2017), David Labaree maps the unfolding of an evolutionary process that yielded the national enterprise in existence today. Describing the American system of higher education as an anomaly, he indicates that to call it a system is generous since it suggests some form of centralized planning with a controlling structure to advance stated objectives. American higher education emerged from an evolutionary process, not designed construction. What does exist resembles a system insofar as there are frameworks that set some normative patterns and common expectations in place, but these are little more than broad boundary conditions more about containment than intent (Labaree 2017).

The origins of the 19th-century college-founding movement emerged through the combined interests of denominational zeal and local economic development, producing myriad small struggling colleges across many parts of the developing United States. Labaree wrote:

> By all rights, this never should have happened. Its origins were remarkably humble: a loose assortment of parochial nineteenth-century liberal arts colleges, which emerged in the pursuit of sectarian expansion and civic boosterism more than scholarly distinction. These colleges had no academic credibility, no reliable source of students, and no steady funding. (Labaree 2017, 1)

Frederick Rudolph, in his classic work *The American College and University: A History* (1962), describes the modest early days for these colleges. He wrote:

> Often when a college had a building, it had no students. If it had students, frequently it had no building. If it had either, then perhaps it had no money, perhaps no professors; if professors, then no president, if a president, then no professors. Perhaps as many as seven hundred colleges tried and failed before the Civil War. (Rudolph 1962, 47)

Though the actual number of colleges founded during this period is disputed by historians, since the existence of a charter did not necessarily result in a sincere attempt to establish an institution, the growth of the college movement was not driven by government design or action. It was regional church leaders and local citizens pursuing their aligned interests that created the necessary conditions.

I identify strongly with this history since my own institution, Central College, was founded in 1853 by the citizens of Pella, Iowa, and the Baptist Education Society of Iowa. Local communities competed to attract the funding available from the Baptist church, and even though the community was founded by immigrants from the Netherlands affiliated with the Dutch Reformed Church, its bid was successful. Sixty-three years later, the Reformed Church in America acquired the college as the Baptist church intended to close it down. In the earliest days, however, as the first president Emmanuel Scarff traveled to Pella from Dayton, Ohio, to assume his new duties, he arrived to discover the facilities were not ready, and the start of school was delayed. Since no furniture for the school was available, the first order of business was to go out and cut down some trees.

Labaree summarized the results of this evolutionary process as follows:

> As we have seen, the system emerged in a time when the state was weak, the market strong, and the church splintered. Its early aims had little to do with first-rate research, high level learning, social mobility, or economic utility. The early colleges, which established the core rules and structures of the system, were set-up to accomplish other less elevated goals, such as to promote sectarian influence, enhance property values, and provide bragging rights for one town over another. The result was a flexible, durable, entrepreneurial, and consumer-oriented system of higher education. But the substantive problem is that this system of higher education did not arise in order to provide education, and for a long time what education it did provide was not very high.

I suggest, however, that these unlikely origins are what have made the American system of higher education so successful. It succeeded by doing everything wrong. It's a system without a plan, which emerged in response to a set of market-based incentives that were peculiar to a particular time and place—the early nineteenth century United States. Since no governing entity had the will, the power, or the money to control its development, the system fumbled along on its own. It learned how to adapt to contingency, take advantage of opportunity, survive in the face of adversity, seek out sources of financial and political support, accumulate a variety of social functions and forms of legitimacy, please major constituencies, and develop a loyal and generous group of alumni. (Labaree 2017, 182)

Understanding this history as it has unfolded through the long arc of time is essential to interpreting the context in which institutions work today. Through the end of the 19th century and the first half of the 20th century, the postsecondary universe expanded and became more sophisticated with the emergence of research universities developed on a European model of higher learning and further animated by the Morrill Land Grant Acts of 1862 and 1890. These acts provided the foundation for public universities to promote technical education on a much larger scale. Through time, these endeavors had stimulating effects on existing colleges as the body of knowledge expanded and expectations for professional life grew. These were challenging days of great incongruity as elite university education for the wealthy began to merge with broader socioeconomic strata including less well-to-do families seeking technical and professional careers. Growth, accompanied by increasing societal complexity, made the university a place of immense ambiguity, but high relevance.

Laurence Veysey, in his text *The Emergence of the American University* (1965), describes an institutional setting in which the expanding scale of the enterprise of higher education created norms that came to define the idea of a system, if not in fact, in practice. He wrote:

> One may well pause to ponder this rapid stylization of institutional relationships. Before 1890 there had been room for decided choice about paths of action; there had been academic programs which differed markedly from one another. . . . During the [eighteen] nineties in a very real sense the American academic establishment lost its freedom. To succeed in building a major university, one now had to conform to the standard structural pattern in all basic respects—no matter how one might trumpet one's few peculiar embellishments. A competitive market for money, students, faculty, and prestige dictated the avoidance of pronounced eccentricities. Henceforth, the initiative had to display itself within the lines laid down by the given system.
>
> The structure of the new American university did not, of course, wholly determine the daily functioning of those who participated in the institution. However, the effects of this structure were clearly relevant to the tenor of American academic life. These effects could be direct, as in all the visible relationships of command, or indirect in terms of expected roles and ways of doing things. Compatible thoughts and activities were rewarded; threatening actions were tacitly or openly punished. Expectations of reward and punishment led to unconscious habit patterns. (Veysey 1965, 340)

The national higher education enterprise was built very slowly, stone by stone. Rudolph and Labaree remind leaders that the original footings for higher learning in America were anything but sure. Yet even in the absence of a design, eventually a foundation was secured in place as norms were established. Trial and error may not be efficient methods, but given enough time and energy, they would prove effective in providing a sturdy platform for further development. Veysey reinforces the understanding that building on that foundation set in place patterns by which the expanding structure could endure. In the absence of design, coherence is found in conformity. It now feels so permanent and impervious to change. The challenge with change in this context, however, is not that it is impossible. Given enough determination, patterns do change. It just takes a lot of time.

Evolving the "System" by Assimilation

The national higher education enterprise continued to evolve through the 20th century and matured despite the immense challenges presented by the Great Depression. This evolutionary process introduced a fundamental shift on the heels of World War II. President Harry S. Truman was leading the country at a time when the wounds of war and the pain of economic collapse were still raw. The GI Bill was adopted in 1944 to accommodate returning veterans. The United Nations was in its infancy. Fears of totalitarianism were pronounced, and global cooperation was high on the agenda. This was a decade before the Russian satellite, Sputnik (1957), circled the globe exacerbating "Cold War" tensions, and several years before the Supreme Court's *Brown v. Board of Education* (1954) decision began reshaping expectations regarding equality. It was a time of immense societal change, complicated significantly by a changing global landscape.

Into this swirling context of societal change, President Truman appointed the Commission on Higher Education in 1946—

the first of its kind. The report of this commission, chaired by George F. Zook, then president of the American Council on Education, was titled *Higher Education for American Democracy*, published in 1947. The full report in six volumes outlined a national agenda for higher education. This is where the system (i.e., pattern) of higher education known today was first imagined. I think of this report as the minutes of the first meeting regarding higher education in the modern era. Sometimes it reads like prophecy. The task of the commission was outlined as follows:

> The President's Commission on Higher Education has been charged with the task of defining the responsibilities of colleges and universities in American democracy and in international affairs—and, more specifically, with reexamining the objectives, methods, and facilities of higher education in the United States in the light of the social role it has to play. (President's Commission 1947, vol. 1, 1)

Part of what added to the potency of the report, however, was an alignment of interests sufficient to overcome dissent. The higher education enterprise, according to the report, already was pursuing important questions regarding the role postsecondary education can and should play in a changing society. The preface to the report continued:

> The colleges and universities themselves had begun this process of reexamination and reappraisal before the outbreak of World War II. For many years they had been healthily dissatisfied with their own accomplishments, significant though they have been. Educational leaders were troubled by an uneasy sense of shortcoming. They felt that somehow the colleges had not kept pace with changing social conditions, that the programs of higher

education would have to be repatterned if they were to prepare youth to live satisfyingly and effectively in contemporary society.

One factor contributing to this sense of inadequacy has been the steadily increasing number of young people who seek a college education. As the national economy became industrialized and more complex, as production increased and national resources multiplied, the American people came in ever greater numbers to feel the need of higher education for their children. More and more American youth attended colleges and universities, but resources and equipment and curriculum did not keep pace with the growing enrollment or with increasing diversity of needs and interests among students. (President's Commission 1947, vol. 1, 1)

The fullness of this agenda was impressive. Outlined in the report are a vast number of recommendations that became a blueprint for the development of postsecondary education for decades. At the macro scale, several key elements set the overall context. At the center was the realization that population growth was coming and the American economy needed to absorb more individuals into the mix. Notably, the report anticipated enrollment in colleges and universities needed to double from the 1947–48 level within a 15-year period. Other imperatives pointed to the impact science and technology would have on society and the workforce, including the advent of the "atomic age," the unavoidable reality that America was set in a global context and would be seeing immigration from around the world, the importance of international cooperation with the founding of the United Nations, and the vital need for diplomacy. The overarching theme, however, was the preservation, spread, and vitality of democracy in the United States and around the world. The social role for higher education was a central focus. The scope of the report extended further to include equal access and opportunity for all, the importance of general education for citizens and its relationship to vocational education, as well as sector-specific recommendations for community colleges, liberal arts colleges, professional schools, graduate schools, funded research, and adult education. Implementation also was forecasted with recommendations related to funding this national enterprise, including student financial aid, support for facilities and infrastructure development, research funding, and the development of faculty staffing.

Given the downstream impact of this report, one would think coordinated government action must have been at the center of a robust process of design and execution. This was not the case. The report stirred controversy and dissent. As originally conceived, the focus of funding was to be directed at public institutions. A Statement of Dissent was published with a report articulating the argument that private institutions also serve a public interest and should be entitled to participate appropriately in publicly funded resources. This argument obviously had merit sufficient to persuade policymakers that both public and private institutions needed to be partners in this vast undertaking.

Independent colleges and universities were not alone in setting forth expressions of concern. John R. Thelin, in his book titled *A History of American Higher Education* (2019), notes, "The Achilles heel of the report was that it moved too far, too fast, in its suggestions for federal involvement in higher education" (Thelin 2019, 269). To some extent this was a matter of federal spending and the considerable commitment of tax dollars implied by the recommendations for building a much larger higher education enterprise. There were also concerns regarding the potential for overreach into state and local policy matters, which at the time (during the late 1940s) included racially segregated public education.

Similar to the late 19th- and early 20th-century evolutionary pattern of development in colleges and universities, the broad-based assimilation process was manifested following WWII, rooted in the themes of the Truman Commission Report. Thelin wrote:

> Although the Truman Commission Report brought the federal government into the nationwide discussion about higher education, it was state governments, private foundations, and individual colleges and universities that took the initiative in the late 1940s and early 1950s to carry out its kinds of recommendations. It was premature, perhaps presumptuous, for the commission to take on a visionary role. (Thelin 2019, 270)

The achievement of the Truman Report was the articulation and dissemination of a set of core principles that would, in time, be assimilated into the patterns of the evolving postsecondary universe. As noted earlier, the report credited institutions of higher education with already being aware "for many years" of the need to change to adequately serve a dynamic society. The report proved useful as a compendium of ideas that aided systemic assimilation through the years. Arguably, this was a process that took about 25 years to fully unfold to a point one might describe as substantial completion of a stated agenda for higher education.

Through the years at the federal level, the evolution was aided by a 1956 report from President Eisenhower's Committee on Education Beyond the High School and by higher education task forces appointed by Presidents Kennedy and Nixon in 1960 and

1969, respectively. These reports focus mostly on the increasing need for funding to support the national expansion of higher education as the population of potential college-aged students swelled. Eighteen years after the Truman Report, the Higher Education Act of 1965 was adopted, which defined the essential federal role in setting expectations, rules, and regulations related to the funding of postsecondary education. As critics of the Truman Report noted, there has been an increasing interest (some would argue intrusion) among federal policymakers in the programs, policies, and procedures of postsecondary institutions. As always, the purse strings can reach far. Still, the federal role is quite limited in its ability to initiate institutional-level change.

Just maintaining limited federal policies related to higher education has proved to be an enormous challenge. The adoption of the Higher Education Act in 1965 was followed by legislative reauthorization in 1968, 1972, 1976, 1980, 1986, 1992, 1998, and 2008. The 2008 reauthorization expired in 2013, and for the past decade the shifting political environment has prevented further legislative action. Many policy adjustments have been made through time by either congressional action or agency rulemaking, but they have been insufficient to advance a broader federal agenda for higher education. There has been no comprehensive action attempted by the federal government in the policy framework connected to higher education since the release of the Spellings Commission report in 2006 and the reauthorization of the Higher Education Act in 2008. Still, a lot of change is happening by assimilation through the myriad channels of influence surrounding and penetrating institutions of higher learning.

Reinterpreting the "System" to Support Change

According to the most recent data available from the *Digest of Educations Statistics* (NCES n.d.a), there are nearly 19 million students enrolled in degree-granting institutions in the postsecondary universe. The number of degree-granting institutions is just under 4,000. Almost 1.5 million faculty members teach students, and when included with staff members, the total employee headcount exceeds 3.8 million. They are together engaged in 58 states and jurisdictions, each with its own set of legal, regulatory, and policy frameworks. They are also guided by one of 19 recognized institutional accreditors and approximately 60 programmatic accreditors. Each of the nearly 4,000 institutions define the relevant programs of study, degree levels, and curricular and cocurricular activities uniquely, yet within broad patterns of conformity, consistency, and accountability. These institutions are classified, ranked, and evaluated by many external entities, each with its own perspective on higher education. There are many conventions and compliance measures informing best practices and expected patterns of behavior.

In chapter 1, I presented three images that help in understanding the characteristics and dynamics shaping national higher education enterprise in general, or colleges and universities in particular. They are like cathedrals in their structural rigidity built through centuries. They are like the Borg in adopting change by collective assimilation over long periods of time. Approaching systems and institutions to initiate change requires a careful assessment of the presenting conditions into which the work of planning will be introduced, similar to building a canal.

The characteristics of the postsecondary universe, noted above, reinforce an understanding that the "system" is enormous and highly complex. The misstep too often taken by policymakers is to assume the process is a straightforward task of building the Suez Canal when the terrain is much more like Panama. Appointing a commission and issuing a report with the belief that it will result in rapid systemic change is the equivalent of landing on the shores of Panama with a shovel and starting to dig a canal. It will not work.

The terrain of higher education, as Labaree noted, is deeply rooted in market-based incentives. The national higher education enterprise is a marketplace in which the competition for resources has been expanding dramatically as they have become increasingly scarce. The expanding cost base for operating institutions has only intensified this reality. I often tell policymakers that institutions collaborate more than compete, and I continue to believe that is true. At the same time, the competitive dynamics are becoming more pronounced as population demographics no longer support the scope of the enterprise at its current scale.

One of my long-serving trustees at Central College had a lifelong career in banking. He also has become a student of higher education through the years. What he has noted is that in many business contexts, the market would care for the excess capacity in the system. Banks that fall on hard times will be absorbed in the system. Though this is not always an orderly process, it is one that is more or less reliable as regulators and banks reinforce stability in the system. He often reminds me higher education lacks underlying systems to facilitate this.

I heard similar comments from a colleague some years ago, who was a professor of economics. His research specialized on the airline industry. At the time, airlines were experiencing considerable financial distress and I asked him if he was concerned about the viability of the industry. He was not at all concerned, noting there is demand from the public, and there are trained personnel, specialized facilities, and dedicated equipment. While specific airlines might not survive in view of the financial conditions, the market would take care of it. Both regulators and industry professionals would sort it out to ensure a sustainable system.

These comments point to the fundamental difference—there is no effective system in higher education that can manage the enterprise on a national scale. To the extent there are regulatory functions, they are of marginal benefit in a system so diffused. There is no entity like the FDIC to appear and facilitate necessary transitions in the postsecondary universe. There are no business leaders who will do the work to facilitate the change process. For example, there have been attempts by both federal and state agencies, as well as accrediting associations, to exert more influence over institutions experiencing distress, but there is little substantive intervention they can apply. The marketplace for students, donors, and grants drives colleges and universities far more than those who would seek to regulate or even guide institutions. Less distressed circumstances also demonstrate the market-based reality of the higher education enterprise. Conventional wisdom drives institutional decision-making at every level. Peer analysis is a dominant force among colleges and universities. Safe harbor for administrators is found in conformity to the prevailing patterns in the industry. This is evidenced in program development, curricular design, student recruitment, administrative practice, fundraising, and financial management, among others.

The inherently rigid structures in the national higher education enterprise that change through the slow process of assimilation are, in the end, driven by uncontrollable market dynamics. The marketplace evolves at a pace faster than the structures or assimilation process will allow. Policymakers, regulators, and association leaders who seek to intervene lack the jurisdiction and tools needed to successfully facilitate change with the pace and scope they desire.

Returning to Labaree's description of the early evolutionary development of colleges and universities, he wrote:

> As with a lot of market-based institutions, it was rigid in its focus on the need to survive, while being quite flexible over the years about how to justify its existence in the face of changing contexts and constituencies. At various times, and all at the same time, it has existed in order to promote the faith, enrich developers, boost civic pride, educate leaders, produce human capital, develop knowledge, provide opportunity, promote advantage, supply a pleasant interlude between childhood and adulthood, help people meet the right spouse, expand the economy, and enhance state power. Oh, and yes, it has also served as a minor league for professional sports, a major venue for public entertainment, and a massive jobs program. (Labaree 2017, 182–83)

Those in lament over the condition of and prospects for higher education today suffer from a lack of understanding about the terrain in which they are seeking to work. They express bewilderment at what they see to be recalcitrance of colleges and universities to change, not understanding the structures they seek to amend were formed over centuries, change by gradual assimilation, and reside in a marketplace with innumerable segments, which no one controls.

The greatest and best hope for higher education is that all collectively realize there is a reason for the present condition.

Remarkably, the approach to the structural realities faced is not to ease the structural pressure but to increase it by inserting even more complex performance demands. Each time another set of expectations is added to the existing structure, it creates more interconnections in the system that simply reinforce and expand the existing structure. Instead of facilitating the inherent process of collective assimilation, leaders often seek to supplant it by assuming abrupt systemic change will erase centuries of history amassed in a vast network of largely autonomous institutions. Misreading this challenging terrain not only risks continued failure of one renovation attempt after another, but it diverts time, energy, and money, with wasted efforts and disappointment.

Arthur Levine and Scott Van Pelt, in their book *The Great Upheaval: Higher Education's Past, Present, and Uncertain Future* (2021), provided an unvarnished analysis of the patterns of change that have occurred through time. They justifiably argued that a process of systemic change is well underway as the industrial revolution gradually gives way to an era of higher education that is yet to be defined. In the preface for their book, they observed there is a split opinion among experts about how change is likely to unfold in the years ahead, comparing those who see change as an incremental process and those who forecast widespread and abrupt disruption. They wrote:

> Recent years have witnessed an outpouring of publications about the future of American higher education, which mirror this split and everything in between. There have been calls for change, pleas for preservation, and visions of what lies ahead, ranging from the utopian to the apocalyptic. Taken as a whole, this writing is largely ahistorical, projecting the future on the basis of what is going on

today and expected future trends rather than examining how we got here and the lessons the past teaches. It also tends to focus on higher education in isolation, ignoring the pressures and changes other knowledge industries experience. It is often rooted in one of the multiplicity of changes occurring in society, usually new technologies. Too often advocacy, what the author wants higher education to become, overshadows the analysis. (Levine and Van Pelt 2021, xi)

Set before leaders is an incredibly rich inheritance to steward for future generations. Doing so requires the acknowledgment that many have been thinking about this the wrong way. Higher education since its earliest days has been managed through the long arc of time. Using that as an advantage is the best chance to preserve and promote this national enterprise.

The Truman Report provided the best clues on how to proceed, given what unfolded in the years that followed. First, the commission acknowledged and commended the higher education community for initiating this work through its expression of dissatisfaction. In other words, the commission was seeking to cooperate with the assimilation energy already being manifested in the national higher education enterprise. Second, it called on the higher education community to pursue something aspirational, namely, "defining the responsibilities of colleges and universities in American democracy." This was a call to a national agenda that brought with it a sense of national duty. Third, the process and the resulting report allowed for dissent. Part of the assimilation process is disagreement, debate, and deliberation. Fourth, the commission, and by extension the president, committed the work to the higher education community, releasing it into its hands as institutions, foundations, and states saw the benefits to be derived through a sustained and collective effort. Consistent with the diffused nature of the system, it was taken up by various players through time—in fact, decades. Upon reflection, the ideas outlined in the report mattered most as they conveyed a sense of opportunity.

The national higher education enterprise will inevitably encounter a very different set of conditions in the coming years. One perspective was offered by my economics colleague who reassured me the airline industry would evolve, and it did. Adopting this perspective, one can argue that whatever the pathway forward, there will be some societal need for higher learning. Demand will persist, though perhaps at a lower level. The work initiated in the 1940s anticipated growth. By contrast, the work of the 2020s may be more about contraction or focus. The system will without a doubt adapt, but not without significant collateral effects. Just as the fledgling institutions did in the 19th century, those that are able will endure and those that are unable will conclude. Such a Darwinian approach appears to be an inevitable path unless a change in perspective is adopted. This is the market-based reality; in the end, it will leave institutions of higher education to their own devices.

Another perspective acknowledges today's societal changes will have systemic impacts on the higher education enterprise. Instead of isolating institutions that risk being stigmatized by the challenges they face, policymakers, associations, and foundations could facilitate healthy interactions by being less threatening. Instead, they could convene the higher education community to formulate a common understanding of what lies ahead, develop a shared vocabulary, foster greater societal understanding, and dial down the anxiety. The incentives for institutional leaders to be guarded about sharing information are significant.

There is a feeling of both personal and professional risk on many levels of leadership. The Truman Report outlined ways in which this diverse enterprise could move forward in a manner consistent with its own interests, but also in the national interest. Such a legacy is, in one sense, a gift and in another sense, a curse. To proceed from here is assured. How to proceed is a matter of choice. Time remains the greatest asset, and managing that arc is the most important responsibility.

CHAPTER 3

Why Can't I Escape?

The first two chapters presented a macro-level view of how change occurs in the postsecondary universe, with downstream effects on institutions. A gradual process of assimilation, marked by periodic spikes in the energy for change, is followed by recursive episodes of conformity to newly established norms. Change management, therefore, must take into consideration the entire landscape of higher education since there is no central authority defining the agenda, tasks, and accountabilities for change. These external conditions reinforce rigidities through compliance with established conventions, and at the same time, cooperate with emergent innovations that inspire duplication and replication across the enterprise. It is by its nature incremental. This process has proved durable through generations. Colleges and universities are, in this respect, products of their environment.

The focus now shifts to the micro-level view, though the dynamics are similar. Applied within the institutional context, the image of the cathedral is a reminder that an organization in the present is an accumulation of its historical foundational elements set in position long ago, the evolving structural features that have guided periods of evolution through generations, and the adornments that have gradually changed through seasons of development. Likewise, the image of the Borg applies as colleges and universities individually assimilate changes under the influence of broad-based conventional wisdom. As they embrace best practices presented by professional colleagues and accept the mandates of regulators, through time, emerging patterns of organization and reorganization are adopted. Yet, like the image of canal building, the landscape into which the new canal is to be built (the organization into which change is introduced) is the primary concern of the leader. The readiness for change is the first and most essential task. If the antecedents for effective change are not well articulated, the process for change not viewed as legitimate within the framework of shared governance, and the time needed for change to be adopted not allowed, then the probability for successful change management is diminished.

The three images each represent unique aspects of the college or university as an organization—they are designed to be sturdy and enduring; they assimilate change through time and create renewed expectations for conformity; and they take time to change given the inherent complexity of the landscape they occupy. No one image is a perfect illustration, but the three serve as helpful interpretive tools when viewing the complex task of leading and managing an institution.

Colleges and universities, therefore, face challenges on two fronts in leading and managing change—the macro-level influences and the micro-level realities. They are set in a context of a fragmented national system that reinforces conformity and compliance with established norms. They are embedded in a complex set of organizational dynamics fraught with ambiguity. Neither the overall national enterprise nor individual institutions of higher education think and act with strict rationality. This is what limits and confounds attempts to manage change. Navigating this terrain is complicated. Creating the conditions for change alone is an arduous task. This is why it benefits leaders to see time as the greatest asset to change and to manage it well. Managing through the arc of time begins with understanding how organizations behave.

Trapped in an Organization

Early in my years of graduate study at Teachers College, Columbia University, I enrolled in a course titled "Organization and Administration of Higher Education." Our professor was Robert Birnbaum, a noted scholar of organizational theory in higher education, who a short time later extended his career at the University of Maryland. He was an engaging teacher, as well as a prolific author. His book *How Colleges Work: The Cybernetics of Academic Organization and Leadership* (1988) was soon to be released, but he permitted us to read his manuscript prior to publication.

Birnbaum was accomplished in the use of classroom activities, relying on games and simulations to illustrate the dynamics of organizations. A section of the course was devoted to exploring the roles and responsibilities of the key stakeholders in a college or university—trustees, administrators, faculty, and students. On one occasion, our class with more than 40 students assembled as usual, but in a different setting. The session was to be devoted to a simulation. Divided into four groups, initially we had no idea what the groupings meant. We were then separated into four rooms and given packets of information and instruction.

In the news at the time was President Ronald Reagan's proposed Strategic Defense Initiative (SDI), also popularly referred to as the "Star Wars" program. It was to be a missile defense system designed to protect the United States from a nuclear attack. The announcement of the initiative in 1983 became the subject of widespread debate and controversy, including on college and university campuses.

Once settled into our respective spaces, we opened our packets of materials to discover we had been assigned to one of the four key stakeholder groups noted above. I was assigned to the group of administrators. The student group was given a specific task to begin the simulation—a roaming protest march railing against our fictional university's funded research activities associated with SDI. Student demands were designed to attract the attention of many outside the university. Birnbaum then left us to our own devices.

As the students agitated and escalated their concerns, the trustees, faculty members, and administrators began to engage in predictable ways. Our administrators sent delegations to meet with each of the constituent groups. The faculty demanded the protection of academic freedom, the trustees wanted to know who was accountable and how this would be resolved, and administrators tried to find a way to placate everyone. Admittedly, the dynamics represented a caricature of higher education as participants played the roles in a stereotypical fashion. The potency of the simulation, however, manifested in two ways. First, the interactions produced complicated effects as reactions from one group informed the subsequent reactions of others, though in ways that tended to produce more conflict. Second, the adoption of stereotypical roles illustrated for us that these constituent groups tend to behave as expected since members of a group are socialized into the perspectives they represent. As the exercise unfolded, it seemed the predictable dynamics were hardwired into our thinking and behavior. In the end, we got nowhere near a resolution, which was, of course, the point.

Conceptions and Misconceptions of Organizations

Birnbaum's class was not about how to organize and manage, though I suspect some of my classmates would have preferred that approach. Instead, the course was about understanding and interpreting the dynamics of organizations. This was a course about applied organizational theory. The theorists he presented to us have been my thought partners since the late 1980s and have served me well through the course of my career. From time to time, I am asked for a reading list by a young administrator or a new trustee. My recommendations typically include works from this list. My purpose in reviewing this literature here is to be of service to those today who express confusion and frustration with what they see happening around them in the organizations they serve. When they are looking for an escape from the organizational traps that ensnare, this collective body of literature provides clues needed to understand and interpret what they are seeing and find a way out.

I trace nearly 80 years of evolving ideas about organizations, all of which remain relevant. It follows a pattern of increasing nuance and acknowledged complexity. The details of each can be explored further in the original works. Thus, my purpose is to make a point: organizations are difficult to define and describe, let alone manage. The expanding ideas contained in the literature of organizational theory bear witness to one simple truth: organizations are messy.

The emergence of early theoretical constructs for modern organizations were first inspired by the industrial revolution, including Max Weber's (1947) concepts of bureaucracy and Fredrick Taylor's (1911) notion of scientific management. These ideas were products of their time. Such frameworks offered a view of organization that reflected a societal transition from an economy of individual farmers, artisans, and merchants to larger-scale organizations and systems supported by mechanization. Organizational systems, like machines, were seen through the lens of interchangeable parts, division of labor, and production lines. Well-ordered organizations sought to adapt humans to systems.

I recently stopped at a neighborhood lemonade stand with about six children involved in the organization. Two were enthusiastically waiving signs on the nearby corner urging passing vehicles to turn onto the side street for a welcome repast on a hot day. Persuaded to make the turn, I was greeted by another advising me of my options, which included lemonade, grape Kool-Aid, and chocolate chip cookies. Another child provided my drink, dedicated to that task, after it had been poured by still another. I handed my money to the remaining young staff member of the stand. Perhaps the children found their way to that organizational design by the patterns they have seen in school, or maybe the supervising parent had a role to play. Whatever the case, it was a classic bureaucracy with specialization of labor, clear rules, and a hierarchy of leadership. The structures of bureaucracy can serve well, as they did in this example, but are limited in effectiveness by the ability, willingness, and predictability of participants in playing their respective roles.

By the middle of the 20th century, Herbert Simon, a noted political scientist, advanced a more nuanced understanding of organizational theory focused on decision-making. His book, *Administrative Behavior: A Study of Decision-Making Processes in Administrative Organization*, originally published in 1945, presented an overlay of human behavior on the structural framework of a bureaucracy by exploring patterns of decision-making. He began by articulating the widely accepted principles of administration at that time:

1. Specialization of the task among the group;
2. Arranging the members of the group in a determinate hierarchy of authority;
3. Limiting the span of control at any point in the hierarchy to a small number;
4. Grouping the workers, for purposes of control, according to (a) purpose, (b) process, (c) clientele, or (d) place. (Simon 1976, 21)

Simon then carefully scrutinized each of these principles and concluded:

Since these principles appear relatively simple and clear, it would seem that their application to concrete problems of administrative organization would be unambiguous, and that their validity would be easily submitted to empirical test. Such, however, seems not to be the case.

None of the four [principles] survived in very good shape, for in each case was found, instead of an univocal principle, a set of two or more mutually incompatible principles apparently equally applicable to the administrative situation.

Can anything be salvaged which will be useful in the construction of an administrative theory? As a matter of fact, almost everything can be salvaged. The difficulty has arisen from treating as "principles of administration" what are really only criteria for describing and diagnosing administrative situations. (Simon 1945, 21, 35–36)

Simon's work represented the broader realization that the complexity of organization does not bend to a rigid theory of administration. Organizations are highly contextual and routinely betray strict formulations of design.

Through time, changing ideas about administration eventually gave rise to theories of organizations more rooted in art than science. For these theorists, the experience of organizational life was better expressed through metaphor, narrative, and culture than systems, structures, and rules. Rationality yielded to ambiguity. Gareth Morgan, a noted organizational theorist and management consultant, authored *Images of Organization* (1986) in which he described organizations variously as machines, organisms, brains, cultures, political systems, psychic prisons, logical constructs, and instruments of dominion. The premise for his work was the idea that

organizations are complex and paradoxical phenomena that can be understood in many different ways. . . . By using different metaphors to understand the complex and paradoxical character of organizational life, we are able to manage and design organizations in ways that we may not have thought possible before. (Morgan 1986, 13)

As metaphors for organizations proliferated, another dimension of interpretation emerged in the form of organizational culture. Whatever image may be applied to describing an organization, the individuals and groups embedded in the organization shape and are shaped by normative patterns of behavior.

Edgar Schein, a professor at the MIT Sloan School of Management, was a theorist who focused his work on understanding organizational behavior and culture. His 1992 book, *Organizational Culture and Leadership*, explored the "hidden and complex aspects of organizational life." Organizational culture is difficult to define as it may be composed of observed behavioral regularities when people interact; group norms; espoused values; formal philosophy; rules of the game; climate; embedded skills; habits of thinking, mental models, and/or linguistic paradigms; shared meanings; and root metaphors or integrating symbols. Regardless of how these various elements of organizational life might be manifested in any one group, something one would think of as a culture within an organization suggests the presence of some structural stability, as well as a pattern or integration of the various elements (Schein 1992, 8–10).

The concept of an organizational culture lacks clear definition and yet, despite its ambiguity, there is a shared sense of understanding among the participants of the normative patterns embedded in the shared experience. Schein frames three levels of culture intended to sort the phenomena represented in a culture into meaningful categories—artifacts, espoused values, and basic assumptions. Schein wrote:

> Though the essence of a group's culture is its pattern of shared, taken-for-granted basic assumptions, the culture will manifest itself at the levels of observable artifacts and shared espoused values, norms and rules of behavior. It is important to recognize in analyzing cultures that artifacts are easy to observe but difficult to decipher and that values may only reflect rationalizations or aspirations. To understand a group's culture, one must attempt to get at its shared basic assumptions and one must understand the

learning process by which such basic assumptions come to be. (Schein 1992, 26)

The available images, metaphors, and cultural references to organizations continued to abound as Lee Bolman and Terrence Deal extended the development of theory in their book, *Modern Approaches to Understanding and Managing Organizations* (1984). Here, they argued that organizations are complex since individual and collective human behavior is unpredictable, surprising because unpredictability pervades the entire organization, deceptive as they often defy expectations and mask realities, and, therefore, are fundamentally ambiguous (Bolman and Deal 1984, 10–12).

More importantly, they introduce interpretive tools useful to organizational leaders in the practice of management, applying four frames or approaches as a means for interpreting organizational phenomena. When confronted with a given condition, a leader can make use of the structural, human resource, political, and symbolic approaches they describe as frames of interpretation. This idea returns us to Simon's earlier assertion that administrative theory is most useful for describing and diagnosing situations. They referred to this practice as reframing, updating, and extending this conceptual framework in a later book titled *Reframing Organizations: Artistry, Choice, and Leadership* (1997). This renewal of their work added more in the way of management practice using the four frames (approaches) and deeper exploration of the nuances contained within each.

The collective work of these theorists is highly relevant to the higher education setting, though none of them were speaking specifically to the college or university as an organization. The next stop in this tour of organizational theory is to apply the ideas offered through the last century to the work of the day. I begin this with the following example.

A Case in Point

The assignment for the project team was to design and implement an enterprise-wide data reporting system for Northeastern University. Early in my time there, beginning in 2000, I served as the director of university planning and research and senior policy advisor to President Richard Freeland. With the lens of institutional research, my contribution was to ensure the needs for reporting and analysis were preserved as this project unfolded. As an administrator with broader interests in the university, however, I was also keen to take into consideration the eventual policy-making and decision-making activities such a system would inform. As noted earlier in chapter 1, through the years I have heard many college and university leaders say, "I am swimming in data, but I have no information." My hope was to improve on that persistent condition.

With plentiful timelines and Gant charts, the tools of project management were on full display. Attending these meetings was often a bit tedious. Most of the time was spent on the specific definitions and characteristics of data elements in the system, including their functional use in supporting the common transactions for university operations—important work, but not particularly inspiring. First and foremost, it was essential we did no harm to the transactional source systems that handled payroll, posted grades, paid vendors, and the like. From time to time, however, we engaged in an extended conversation about the needs for policy analysis and the ways in which the administration of data would support critical decision-making. The IT project manager leading this effort, often impatient with such conversations, one day said in frustration, "Listen, we can get this project done on time and on budget as long as we don't have any more bright ideas." That sincere, albeit misguided assertion has stayed with me ever since—a classic means-end reversal. In the end, the project did not succeed. More interesting is that the effort was preceded by an even more ambitious attempt to create a reporting system and followed by a third more modest project that both ended in complete failure. The three initiatives taken together spanned a decade of time and involved expenditures well into six figures, not including the time spent by participants.

This kind of means-end reversal is repeated frequently across the landscape of higher education. It reminds me of the old saw regarding the surgeon who completed a surgical procedure and reported to the waiting family, "The operation was successful. The patient died." Through an overreliance on structures, systems, procedures, and processes, tasks are completed and boxes checked, but these do not deliver successful, meaningful, and lasting change. I continue to encounter leaders and managers today whose administrative practice is a better fit for the late 19th rather than the early 21st century. I witness fervent dedication to the structural and procedural aspects of organizational management but observe bewilderment at the hidden dynamics of human interaction that confound such rational thinking. Many have no language or vocabulary for understanding or interpreting the hidden aspects of postsecondary institutions, which are often exceedingly complex. Constituent or stakeholder groups have widely divergent views of what aspirations and activities should be pursued.

The development of organizational theory has benefits in seeking to define, describe, and diagnose situations in organizations. The myriad images, metaphors, narratives, and interpretive frameworks have much to offer. Yet a leader is left with the realization that however one chooses to characterize an organization, there is one fundamental quality that washes over all of them: ambiguity.

Embracing Ambiguity

It is a natural instinct to rationalize organizations through administrative systems, whether it is a lemonade stand, an IT project, or an entire institution. Doing so makes obvious sense. Leaders rely on the structures of bureaucracy for purposes of ordering tasks, making assignments, setting expectations for deliverables, and establishing accountabilities. Bureaucracies are necessary to foster discipline in support of a shared task. The error is the assumption that the application of administrative systems should be sufficient to achieve the intended results. Unfortunately, when these systems break down, the tendency is to blame the people involved for noncompliance, inadequate performance, or even malevolence. If organizational theory teaches us anything, it teaches us that bureaucracies are necessary but insufficient for leading organizations. At their best, they are little more than a façade. At their worst, they are a fiction. The real work of advancing an organization is found in all that undergirds and surrounds the bureaucratic structures used. Michael Cohen and James March provided insights into this work 50 years ago.

At the time *Leadership and Ambiguity* (1974) was published, Michael Cohen was a professor at the University of Michigan and James March was a professor at Stanford University. Though the book was written with specific reference to the college and university presidency, it remains highly relevant to all those invested in the higher education enterprise. Early in my career, conversations among administrators often referenced a particular chapter in this book. I rarely hear it referenced today; when I ask younger administrators, most are unaware of this classic work. The chapter is titled "Leadership in an Organized Anarchy." It should be required reading for any who aspire to leadership in higher education.

Describing an institution of higher learning as an organized anarchy may seem insulting, but it is an honest appraisal of higher education as a national enterprise, and of individual colleges and universities. The foundational principles Cohen and March offer are the ambiguities of anarchy. There are four:

The Ambiguity of Purpose
The Ambiguity of Power
The Ambiguity of Experience
The Ambiguity of Success

These combined ambiguities result in an organized anarchy. The broad expression of *purpose* may have limited rhetorical value. Yet when subjected to the scrutiny of stakeholders seeking a more precise definition, little agreement will be found beyond vague platitudes. Symbols reign supreme in this context. The identity of any individual or group within the organization omitted from an articulation of purpose will quickly be the subject of criticism.

Power in an organization is a matter of perspective. Many associate power with authority, perhaps in the role of the president or governing board. Power, however, is ambiguous since accomplishing anything of substance in an organization requires willing participation by its members. Power is more often expressed through shared responsibility than direct authority and, therefore, is to some extent a social construct manifested through pattern-like symbols in process rituals, norms, and conventions.

Experience is subjective. The effects of a decision or action taken within the organization are interpreted differently by different individuals or groups. The inherent complexity of organizations, in which many actors shape and influence the decisions made and the actions taken, results in impacts that are ambiguous. Information is also limited within the organization depending on the role one plays. One of my early mentors emphasized that in organizations, sometimes people will believe A + B = D. In such situations I am reminded that Taoist philosophy teaches us, "Those who know do not speak. Those who speak do not know." The result is that the experience of the same situation will be interpreted differently by different people.

Measures of *success* are likewise highly subjective. Members of a campus community will assess accomplishments with very different criteria in mind. Achieving the overall goal of a fundraising campaign may be viewed as successful by some and a failure by others depending on the direction of those funds. Likewise, a governing board may see a president as successful in view of certain criteria whereas a faculty may view the president as a failure based on other criteria. The reverse can also be true.

Based on these characteristics of ambiguity, Cohen and March identify five major properties of decision-making in an organized anarchy.

1. Most issues, most of the time, have *low salience* for most people. Decisions to be made within the organization secure

only partial and erratic attention from participants in the organization. A major share of the attention devoted to a particular issue is tied less to the content of the issue than to its symbolic significance for individual and group esteem.

2. The total system has *high inertia*. Anything that requires a coordinated effort of the organization in order to start is unlikely to be started. Anything that requires a coordinated effort of the organization in order to be stopped is unlikely to be stopped.

3. Any decision can become a *garbage can* for almost any problem. The issues discussed in the context of any particular decision depend less on the decision or problems involved than on the timing of their joint arrivals and the existence of alternative arenas for exercising problems.

4. The processes of choice are easily subject to *overload*. When the load on the system builds up relative to its capabilities for exercising and resolving problems, the decision outcomes in the organization tend to become increasingly separated from the formal process of decision.

5. The organization has a *weak information base*. Information about past events or past decisions is often not retained. When retained, it is often difficult to retrieve. Information about current activities is scant. (Cohen and March 1974, 206–7)

To illustrate how these properties of decision-making are manifested in a college or university given the characteristics of ambiguity, I offer the example of a typical strategic planning process. Whatever its design, most planning processes seek to be comprehensive in scope, structurally sound, symbolically rich, politically palatable, reasonably achievable, relevant to donors, and timebound. Planning typically begins with *low salience* since episodes of planning are a predictable part of institutional life, and most expect its imperatives to be benign or at least non-threatening. The recursive nature of this process rests first on the legitimacy of process evidenced by the participation of acceptable representatives from the various stakeholder groups. If the process appears normative, then salience will remain low despite rhetorical claims that the process is to be a defining moment in the institution's history. A heightened state of alert in approaching a planning process requires a set of antecedent conditions raising the specter of change beyond normal expectations. Such conditions might include a financial crisis, a new presidency, interventions by state policymakers, and the like.

High inertia is a close cousin to low salience since both require some animating force to sponsor a change in posture. The low salience of a routine planning effort will likely maintain inertia by keeping the institution at rest, comfortable with a process that may help to coordinate existing work, encourage modest levels of innovation and creativity, and attract further resources. It takes little coordinated effort to begin planning, and a thoughtful effort in setting up the process is usually sufficient to overcome the inertia present in the organization.

As a planning process unfolds, the intended categories outlined for the planning process are of no real importance. The conversation roams widely as a new idea is easily tied to an existing concern that quickly becomes an issue that needs to be resolved if the aspirations of the plan are to be achieved. The *garbage can* effect is impressive to watch. It is said that any conversation on a campus that lasts long enough will eventually turn to a discussion about parking. I would add if students are involved, the deliberations drift into food service in addition to parking.

The system gets *overloaded* easily in planning since the agenda-setting character of planning is divorced from downstream decision-making processes. One hopes there is alignment between the two, but in some cases, ambition exceeds resource capacity and the patterns and timing of institutional decisions may not align with the aspirations of the plan. An overly ambitious plan, which is more common than one might think, has a higher probability of overloading the system.

One of my mentors was fond of saying if you have 40% of the information you want to make a decision, you are doing well. I'm not sure I agree, though I appreciate the sentiment. A *weak information base* is a common feature in planning. Accordingly, leaders tend to overestimate short-term trends and underestimate long-term trends since the information available is so limited. The data at hand, whether quantitative or qualitative, are subject to interpretation and accordingly carry a degree of ambiguity. Making plans adaptable through time is one way of coping with this, but there is also considerable incentive to ensure a plan is flexible at the outset and not confining. This tends to produce a vague quality in the articulation of the objectives that, in turn, reinforces both *low salience* and *high inertia*.

Seen as a whole, these five properties of decision-making outline the contours of organizational dynamics that are describable and to some degree predictable. The properties also are evident in situations where an extreme set of conditions is presented. The best example in recent memory was the impact the COVID-19 pandemic had on postsecondary institutions. This is a helpful counterexample to the routine planning process described above. As the pandemic fully emerged in March 2020, planning was set aside as crisis management emerged. Quite suddenly, the *salience* of the decision-making activities was high, and *inertia* flipped as the external forces of a public health emergency set campuses in motion that also was quite hard to stop. For example, even as the pandemic waned in 2022, there remained strong voices pressing for vaccination requirements and mask mandates, arguing for what some considered an unsustainable perpetual state of heightened alert. As deliberations unfolded, the range of interconnected issues presented would have filled any conceptual *garbage can* imaginable. The system was completely *overloaded*, and accurate *information* to support decision-making was scarce and quick to change. Accordingly, these five properties in my experience have been reliable as a framework of thinking about leadership in an organized anarchy whether the conditions are normal or novel.

Cohen and March extend the application of the four identified ambiguities and the five properties of decision-making to a set of rules to guide leaders in this anarchical context (Cohen and March 1974). I have rehearsed these many times in my career, though not in a slavish manner. These are, as noted throughout this chapter, ways of describing and diagnosing presenting conditions.

Rule 1: *Spend Time*. Time is the most important asset for leadership since time and energy interact. Shorter timeframes demand higher levels of energy. Energy management is a key function of an organizational leader. Time is also key to leadership since it takes time to learn about what is happening and it takes time to see how organizational phenomena unfold.

Rule 2: *Persist*. The presentation of an issue before the institution may not be resolved in a single attempt. Change management often requires a recursive process of incrementally advancing key portions of a more comprehensive initiative.

Rule 3: *Exchange Status for Substance.* For most people, most issues have low salience. What is more important is the status associated with participation or even leadership in addressing the concerns of the day. Some are politically motivated while others may be the keepers of symbols. Simply being at the table can have higher salience than the topic at hand.

Rule 4: *Facilitate Opposition Participation.* In view of the ambiguities resident in institutions of higher education, the idea that structural authority, absent a crisis, can advance the pursuit of an ambition or resolve a matter of concern is misguided. Bringing those with differing points of view to the decision-making process reduces concerns that the perspectives of detractors are not permitted access to the deliberations. Advancing an interest can be accomplished with the loyal opposition engaged in the work.

Rule 5: *Overload the System.* To some this rule seems counter to the risk identified in the properties of decision-making and may appear cynical as if overloading the system can serve as a distraction for detractors. For me, this goes back to energy management. The expanse of interests present in colleges and universities is enormous. I have been told the experience of feeling overwhelmed can take two forms in which one is energizing and the other debilitating. The challenge is to manage energy properly. In advancing initiatives, a well-loaded system is more productive and efficient.

Rule 6: *Provide Garbage Cans.* This is simply a matter of facilitating the inevitable. Conversations among members of the organization will naturally drift. In more recent years I have heard this referenced as a "parking lot" to avoid diversion and distraction. Regardless of the metaphor employed, the practice of organizing deliberations in avoiding garbage can decision-making is a sound exercise.

Rule 7: *Manage Unobtrusively*. Attempts at tight control of organizational dynamics are a fruitless effort. Organizations have a way of moving on their own, and seeing that is easier at a distance. For me, this is about cooperating with what has been and is going on already. Providing pathways, managing symbols, and rehearsing narratives serve to guide rather than control. There is plenty of opportunity for authority to be expressed when and where appropriate, but much can be accomplished by maintaining an abiding presence, speaking when the voice of leadership will be heard, and acting when the conditions are right.

Rule 8: *Interpret History*. Colleges and universities are rich with history given the length of time most have been in existence. An authentic interpretation is certainly fact based and honest. There is also a narrative quality found in connecting events through time. This tells a story that incorporates the fullness of the challenges and triumphs in addition to articulating the enduring values that have informed that history. This serves to center people in the knowledge that they are part of a larger story.

Cohen and March share many insights into the dynamics of leadership worth exploring in greater detail. As theorists, their analysis of organizational dynamics in postsecondary institutions continues to ring true even after five decades.

Applying Organizational Theory as a Practitioner

For me, organizational theory is a playground of ideas. It has little to do with accuracy since organizations can't effectively be defined individually or collectively. Theory helps to describe and diagnose situations using images, metaphors, and narratives.

The application of theory in this book is based on the three images I have offered: cathedrals, the Borg, and canal building. The theoretical underpinnings of the images are useful as descriptors and the interpretation of conditions. As our theorists have demonstrated, the images represent ideas, perhaps even patterns. What they are not and cannot be are templates. My reference to cathedrals might for some conjure an image of something immovable, but that is not what I have argued. The relevance of the cathedral image is about time, not space. A cathedral is built across generations who each contribute to the development of the whole. The recursive process of change by assimilation and conformity represented in the Borg is also a reference to time as assimilation is not copying but is instead an activity of sorting and experimenting that takes time. Canal building is also a reference to time as the antecedent conditions needed to pursue a course of substantive change must be considered before digging in. Some complain the urgency of the moment demands quick action. I simply point to the consistent failure rate of untimely and rushed processes for change that in the end take more time and cost more in resources. If the time was invested at the outset to realistically consider the presenting conditions, then the results would likely be more satisfying.

I am arguing for a revival of meta-analysis among practitioners in higher education. Prescriptive and simplistic administrative behaviors, devoid of a conceptual understanding and nuanced application of organizational theory, are destined to rehearse patterns in which there is frenetic activity but few results. The visible and tangible structures undergirding higher education often ignore the unseen dimensions of human tendency. The fundamental flaw is that people set in the framework of a group or organization do not always behave as one might predict. This is known intuitively, and theoreticians have further articulated that intuition. That counsel and advice is often ignored, however, as leaders go through the motions of fast-paced process, despite the lack of success. This is why it is so difficult to escape the trap. But the trap is avoidable, and escape is possible, if leaders are willing to devote time and energy to pursuing change in a way that cooperates with what is already happening.

CHAPTER 4

The Six-Pack of Change

During a retreat of the Central College Board of Trustees in 2014, our chair at the time, Lanny Little, displayed the following quotes on the projection screen:

> There is a high likelihood that this year will be a decisive year in the history of Central College.
>
> The decade ahead will be a time of maturity for the college, in which the institution faced up not only to its real financial pressures but also to its identity for the future.
>
> Private colleges in Iowa are in serious trouble. I don't foresee any wholesale failures and closings, but I think we can expect, in many instances, a gradual erosion of quality in which many programs will be reduced to mediocrity.
>
> If quality education is provided, the dollars will come, but an excessive concern for dollars may blind the college to irretrievable losses. It is not enough for Central College to keep its head above water. We must also find our way to a distant shore.

This identity of knowing what an institution is and where's it's going with solid programs in special areas can be the real solution for private colleges.

While some small colleges are turning to focus exclusively on career objectives in an effort to survive, Central should maintain its strong liberal arts character as a means of helping students to successful careers.

Central's immediate goals are the raising of additional funds and the recruitment of students. More efforts will also be made towards the retention of students. Faculty needs to be particularly supportive of students in dealing with their uncertainties, hoping to keep them in or return them to college.

Money and enrollment are the primary responsibility of the administration, with support from the faculty. Long range solutions in maintaining and improving the quality of education must be the primary responsibility of the faculty, with support from the administration.

We need to develop a confidence in our future which will cause people to look at us from the outside and see and institution that is not struggling to survive, but striving to serve, effectively and joyously.

Once the attendees had a moment to read and digest the text, he asked them who they thought uttered the words displayed. After a measured silence one responded, "those are Mark's words." Others agreed. He then reported to them the quotes came from one of my predecessors, Ken Weller, offered during an opening day presentation to the faculty and staff, and later reported in the alumni magazine in 1974 (*Central College Bulletin* 1974). I heard one of the trustees whisper, "And so it will ever be." Too often we think our circumstances are unprecedented.

As Mark Twain reminded us, "History never repeats itself, but it does often rhyme."

In the twilight of his career, I had the privilege of hearing George Keller speak during a conference session at the Society for College and University Planning (SCUP). Often referred to as the "father of strategic planning in higher education," Keller shared reflections on his work to promote strategic management in the college and university landscape. His book, *Academic Strategy: The Management Revolution in American Higher Education* (1983), became standard reading. He advocated for data analysis and forecasting, borrowed the practice of SWOT analysis from industry, and explored ways in which institutions were beginning to adopt new approaches. In particular, he foretold of serious demographic concerns facing higher education and the attending consequences. He wrote,

> A specter is haunting higher education: the specter of decline and bankruptcy. Experts predict that between 10 percent and 30 percent of America's 3,100 colleges and universities will close their doors or merge with other institutions by 1995. On many campuses the fear of imminent contraction or demise is almost palpable. . . . The specter lurks in colleges and universities of all sizes, public as well as private, although smaller private colleges and the academically weaker state colleges and community colleges are widely expected to be the worst hit. (Keller 1983, 3)

Skeptics would argue Keller was wrong. Like other predictions of systemic failure, the reality turned out to be less intense than the forecast suggested. I would argue he wasn't wrong. He was instead successful in giving voice to the emerging challenges, providing insights into how to address them, and offering tools to support the effort. In this sense, Keller's clarion call was heeded by those in a position to act.

I began my career in higher education as an admission counselor in 1983, just as Keller's book was published. The experience of being an admission professional during those years was consistent with Keller's depiction. The discourse within the profession was filled with anxiety; the rise of initiatives to increase participation rates of graduating high school students was robust. Added to this were strategies to develop more program opportunities for adult learners, particularly for degree completion at extension centers in evening and weekend formats. International student recruitment intensified to widen the pool of prospective students. While some institutions still closed or merged, the number was not nearly as high as forecasts suggested. Keller's legacy, however, was the establishment of an enduring framework of strategic thinking within the higher education context. Of note are five domains of forecasting Keller advocated institutions should regularly pursue: *technological, economic, demographic, politico-legal,* and *sociocultural* (Keller 1983, 158).

Through the years I have adapted Keller's approach—to what I call the *Six-Pack of Change*—as a means for refining and extending the conversation about strategy. The six vectors of change include *demographic decline, economic uncertainty, workforce expectations, technological innovation, societal norms,* and *public policy.* These six elements have distinctive characteristics but behave unpredictably as they easily spill into each other, adding to the ambiguity of the enterprise. As tools of interpretation, not unlike images in organizational theory, they can assist in understanding the external terrain, taking into consideration the inherent rigidities and the process of assimilation associated with managing change in our institutions. They, however, cannot provide a road map since they are highly contextual by institution, sector, and region. The nuances of interpretation matter as evidenced in a theory-based view of organizations described and diagnosed by many images, metaphors, and narratives outlined in the previous chapter.

George Keller and Ken Weller, a decade apart, pointed to the realities they faced 40 and 50 years ago, respectively. Throughout my career, this pattern has been rehearsed and reverberates today. It may not exactly repeat, but it rhymes.

Demographic Decline

I was born in 1960, but I was raised in the 1950s. Looking back I realize my experiences were shaped as much by the years preceding my arrival as those that followed. Living on the trailing edge of the baby boom generation provided me with a unique vantage point on shrinking population demographics and the consequential economic and workforce effects manifested through time. The population within my age group, and those that followed, were receding from the peak of the baby boom and the effects were transparent. A few years after I enrolled in kindergarten at the Broad Street School in Endicott, New York, the facility was converted into an office building. Not long after I attended the Henry B. Endicott (HBE) School during my junior high years, it, too, was eventually converted into an office building. There were not enough children being born in the community to support these schools, and consolidation was the order of the day. Through time, neither of these converted schools survived as office buildings; both endured years of vacancy. The downstream economic consequences due to demographic decline and workforce availability have taken their toll. HBE is now an apartment building.

The collateral effects also are pronounced. As the founding place of IBM and Endicott-Johnson Shoes, Endicott boasted a thriving business community with a large workforce. The population of the village swelled to more than 20,000 in 1950. By 1960, it dropped to just under 19,000. The most recent census places the population at 13,668 (USCB 2020). The story of the community I grew up in is one of shrinking population due to both declining fertility rates and a loss of workforce presence. The remnants of Endicott-Johnson Shoes were acquired in the 1990s by another company and relocated out of state. In more recent years IBM closed the last of its facilities, completing a gradual exodus that began when I was in high school. No one planned or designed these changes. They emerged through years of evolution animated by independent actors outside anyone's control.

The same experience has followed me through my years of college and my subsequent career in higher education. I did not fully understand what was unfolding around me in the early years of my professional life, until I heard Keller speak. During his presentation at the SCUP conference, Keller reminded us of the quote commonly attributed to Auguste Comte, "Demography is destiny."

The US Congressional Budget Office (CBO) relies heavily on demographic analysis to determine the long-term impacts of policymaking. In a report titled, *The Demographic Outlook: 2023 to 2053*, the authors note:

> The total fertility rate remains at 1.66 births per woman through 2023 and then rises as fertility rates among women ages 30 to 49

increase. By 2030, the fertility rate is projected to be 1.75 births per woman, where it remains through 2053. That rate is below the replacement rate of 2.1 births per woman—the fertility rate required for a generation to exactly replace itself in the absence of immigration. (CBO 2023)

According to the CBO, the demographic challenges for postsecondary education will remain with us for many years to come. There are, of course, caveats in interpreting these data. First, the CBO could simply be wrong about the future birthrate assumed for American society, though the downward trend is clear and fell below the replacement rate in 2008, where it remains. There is little to suggest this pattern will reverse. Second, an increase in immigration could swell the adult population, as well as the birthrate. However, the geopolitical dynamics pressing against immigration, as well as the US politically partisan reality currently impeding any meaningful attempts at comprehensive immigration reform, make immigration an unlikely source for growing the US population.

As applied more specifically to the postsecondary context, much has been written about the "demographic cliff" forecasting a precipitous further decline in the number of high school graduates beginning in 2026. Most leaders rely on projections from the *Knocking at the College Door* report released periodically by the Western Interstate Commission on Higher Education (WICHE 2020) and projections prepared by the National Center for Education Statistics (NCES) in the *Digest of Education Statistics* (NCES n.d.a) and more specifically the report, *Projections of Education Statistics to 2028* (NCES n.d.b). Building on these data, analysts (Grawe 2018; McGee 2015) have drawn attention to more than just the raw number of high school graduates in the potential candidate pool, but the probability of participation in postsecondary education and persistence to complete a degree. Grawe, in particular, has noted the demographic composition of the emerging pool will have a higher portion of lower-income students and an increase in historically underrepresented students.

Coupled with the more limited tendency of these populations to enroll in college, perceptions of the desirability of college attendance also are changing. Gallup reported in 2023 only 36% of Americans express confidence in higher education, down from 57% in 2015 and 48% in 2018. This trend is reflected in a broader lack of confidence in other institutions in American society (Brenan 2023). Concurrently, in 2023 Gallup reported 71% of current college students enrolled as undergraduates agree or strongly agree that the degrees they are pursuing are worth the price they are paying; just 8% express some level of disagreement (Marken and Hrynowski 2023).

This points to a sustained downward pressure on enrollment that will likely last more than 30 years into the future. As noted in chapter 2, the situation more than 70 years ago was the exact opposite. The United States was anticipating a burgeoning population following World War II and an increasing level of demand for postsecondary education in that population. That pattern shifted in the mid- to late-1980s toward a boom-and-bust cycle that peaked in 2010. Since then, the higher education community has grappled with an overall decline in enrollment that will intensify through the remainder of this decade. It is conceivable the situation could restabilize at lower population levels during the 2030s and beyond, but there are too many variables in play to predict at this stage. The cascading and collateral effects, however, need to be managed as time unfolds. The college founding movement and land grant university expansion of the 19th and early 20th centuries, amplified further by the post–World War II era, will gradually give way to a 21st-century reality of lower population and an uncertain level of demand.

Economic Uncertainty

In the summer of 1983, I was an eager young admission counselor invited to attend a meeting of faculty and staff members of the institution I served. I graduated that year with a Bachelor of Arts in philosophy from Nyack College and was then hired to serve on the admission team with all the typical responsibilities for student recruitment. The president of Nyack College, David Rambo, and the chair of the Board of Trustees, Donald Siebert, addressed our assembly as enrollment pressures mounted and entering class sizes were in decline. Consultants had been hired to rethink the college's marketing strategy, and retention experts were on hand to discuss ways in which the college could increase persistence and graduation rates.

When I entered the college a few years earlier, in 1977, my first-year expenses for tuition, fees, and room and board totaled $3,100. As a student from an economically modest background, I qualified for the maximum Basic Educational Opportunity Grant (BEOG), now known as the Pell Grant, and a full grant from the State of New York under the Tuition Assistance Program, known commonly as a TAP Grant. When those awards were combined with the Francis Asbury Palmer Scholarship I received from the college, I paid nothing out of pocket to enroll in the college.

Seated in the meeting room, which was a section of the dining hall, I listened as renewed energy and enthusiasm were conveyed to us by the college's leadership. I was onboard immediately.

When offered the opportunity to ask questions, I raised my hand and asked, "Our total cost of attendance next year will exceed $10,000. Are we concerned that we might out-price the market?" Siebert, who was the chairman and CEO of the J. C. Penney Company, looked briefly at me, waived his hand, and said, "Everyone has prices." He then moved on to the next question without further comment. It turns out Siebert wasn't wrong, at least not at that time.

The economics of higher education have been a puzzle for decades. On the expense or cost side, colleges and universities suffer from the Baumol effect, also known as cost disease. Simply described, the effect is manifested when costs, particularly labor, increase inexorably in the absence of a gain in productivity. The classic example given is a string quartet. The number of musicians needed to play a string quartet piece is the same today as it was centuries ago. Setting the Baumol effect in the context of higher education, a typical student-to-faculty ratio at an institution is likely today to be the same as it was years ago. What can change that is a gain in productivity by educating more students more efficiently, perhaps with the use of online technologies, for example. Some argue this is the equivalent of listening to a string quartet play by a recording, which represents maximal productivity, but is a different kind of experience. Experiencing a live performance by expertly trained musicians in an acoustically suitable concert setting comes with a much higher cost structure and at a much higher ticket price. Any enterprise that has highly trained personnel with a limited scope of productivity manifests cost disease. Typical examples include professional firms such as doctors, lawyers, and dentists. Faculty and administrators on college campuses are similar. Arguments for increasing productivity abound even as the pressure for the quality of the experience persists. Doctors under managed care regimes have limited time to provide care, sometimes to the consternation of patients. Reliance on physician assistants and nurse practitioners for some services is also a cost intervention designed to increase productivity. Lawyers may rely on trained staff or artificial intelligence to realize productivity gains.

The price side of this consumer relationship is largely unrelated to the cost side. When I enrolled in college, the question of affordability focused almost entirely on the ability to pay the price set before me. As cost disease, coupled with competitive pressures, further exacerbated by declining student demand become more pronounced, the ability to pay the price has given way to the willingness to pay the price. The net price with the application of student aid, now largely in the form of unfunded tuition discounts, has eroded to the point that institutions cannot fund the cost of operation on a decreasing level of net revenue. The reality now is that the sticker price and the net price are no longer helpful in understanding the revenue picture at a college or university. The market price—the average price students are willing to pay—is the best indicator of institutional pricing power.

As many have noted, costs are expanding dramatically, especially given the level of service, amenity, program, and activity expected by the marketplace. Simultaneously, price tolerance is at least static, if not contracting, given broad inflationary pressures and limited disposable family income. Competitiveness in this market can be expressed as follows:

$$\text{Value} = \text{Perceived Quality} / \text{Net Price}$$

For postsecondary institutions, this equation is in one sense a value proposition in a competitive market. It is in another sense a cost model as the value demanded implies a quality of life that cannot be supported by the net price or, better expressed, the market price. This was brought home to me when I learned of a conversation that took place between my vice president for enrollment, Chevy Freiberger, and an admitted student who earned one of our donor-funded full-tuition scholarships. Upon hearing the news he had been awarded the scholarship, the student replied, "That's great! Is there more?"

Analysts have argued for years this condition set is unsustainable. I agree. Despite Siebert's correct assertion in the early 1980s that "everyone has prices," these trend lines have curved with the arc of time. Given aggressive increases in tuition discounting against artificially high tuition pricing, net revenue is declining at a rate that cannot support the structural cost base for an increasing number of colleges and universities.

Workforce Expectations

Through the years I have served on various cross-sector, state-level committees, commissions, councils, and boards. Uniformly, the agenda is about building and sustaining a talented workforce. One of these was a well-funded state initiative to promote STEM education across the spectrum of education levels—primary, secondary, and tertiary. The organization is called the Iowa Governor's STEM Advisory Council, and I had the pleasure of serving on that body for 10 years. While there was some acknowledgment of the benefits of scientific literacy to support effective citizenship, the thrust of the activity was on building a workforce competent in science, technology, engineering, and math. During one meeting I sat next to Kacia Cain, an award-winning and well-regarded high school biology teacher. The presenter for the session before us detailed results of a longitudinal assessment project designed to track persistence of students pursuing STEM-related courses through the years of primary and secondary schooling. A slide appeared on the screen depicting a trend line with a downward curve through time. It informed the council of a declining pattern associated with participation in STEM courses as students age. Of particular note was a steep drop beginning around ninth grade. As I studied the chart, I leaned over to Kacia and asked, "Why does that line curve?" She replied, "Because it gets hard."

During a break we were able to discuss my question further and she explained that STEM education in the lower grades has a lot to do with play. It's very active, hands-on, project focused, and team based. Through time the content demands come with increasing need for individual competency in math and the accompanying analytic skills. It's just the nature of the disciplines. The broad societal benefits for STEM education are obvious, as an evolving economy will rely more on advanced technology and technical skill. The disconnect is that policymakers do not look to the students to understand the future workforce pipeline. They look to the demand for workers in industry.

Overlapping with my years of service on the STEM Advisory Council, I also served on a related council known as Future Ready Iowa. This was a natural extension of the STEM work but was focused entirely on building the workforce for employers in the state. What struck me most through months of deliberation was the idea that students would naturally find their way to "high-demand fields" by raising awareness of the opportunity and providing student aid to support their study and preparation. These are worthy efforts, of course. The problem is no one is talking to the students about their ambitions and interests. Many of these high-demand fields require specific academic preparation and professional promise, as well as dedication, focus, and discipline to obtain the appropriate credentials. My constant refrain is that in the end, students get to choose. They must want to pursue these career pathways.

In November 2021, the Pew Research Center reported the results of a survey focused on the gender gap in college completion. While the gender effects were interesting and important, the overall results shed some light on the misalignment between the expectations of policymakers and industry leaders versus potential students. Respondents who had not completed a college degree were asked why they made that decision and given multiple reasons to consider. As one would expect, affordability was the highest factor, followed by the need to support family. Just below the levels of these responses, however, the report noted 29% indicated they "Just didn't want to," 23% responded they "Didn't need more education for the job/career you wanted," and 20% reported they "Just didn't consider it" (Parker 2021). The issues underlying these results run deep. Enrollment in higher education nationally is trending down, which could involve some lingering post-pandemic effects.

Something more systemic and enduring may be emerging that differs markedly from the post–World War II societal context that gave rise to the higher education enterprise known today. The intent to pursue a college education certainly included a desire to enrich individual career and economic opportunities, but it was also widely perceived as a foundation for producing a broadly educated workforce and an engaged citizenry. A more subtle dimension was the conferring of social status within the professional class. Today that framework for assessing the benefits of a college education has eroded as the price for attendance has increased significantly and the perceived long-term benefits are overtaken by more immediate and practical interests.

Technological Innovation

I am of the generation that grew up with a corded rotary-dial phone, black-and-white television, vinyl records, and a transistor radio. As the computer age arrived in my world, I played the first home television video game called Pong, released in 1975. The first computer form letter I crafted was on a mainframe using a dumb terminal, which necessarily included coding to denote line breaks and page breaks. With the advent of the personal computer and the MS-DOS system that supported the software, WordPerfect, I marveled when I typed and text automatically wrapped at the end of each line. I used an early email system called Jove and reviewed the entire contents of the new World Wide Web on an early web browser known as Mosaic. The first "portable" computer I used weighed about 15 pounds, and my first cell phone was larger than the walkie-talkie I had as a kid.

During the 1980s, technology dominated strategic planning. There was deep concern that the initial acquisition of equipment would require considerable capital investment before returning immense savings to budgets. The need for training was a dominant theme as fearful faculty and administrators expressed concern about students outpacing campuses in their demand for technology. For those years technology was not a tool, it was a strategy. It had to be.

For most of my career the constant refrain was that one day computer technology would save institutions loads of money. It was simply necessary to reach the tipping point. Alas, such a dream was never realized. Technology has been, and always will be, an escalating cost as one generation of technology is supplanted by another.

When I arrived as the new president of Central College in 2010, technology remained a dominant theme as was the case across the higher education landscape. A campus-wide initiative was born years earlier known as "One Port per Pillow." It was all about ethernet. To be attractive to students, my institution, like many across the country, ran ethernet cabling all over campus. The One Port per Pillow project provided a dedicated ethernet connection for each student in the residence halls to connect a computer, as well as a dedicated telephone in each residence hall room. By 2010, Wi-Fi ascended, rendering ethernet the status of wall insulation. At about this time, a question surfaced regarding the use of phones placed in every residence hall room as cell phones also were becoming ubiquitous. An informal inquiry revealed that most phones were located on a closet shelf with the cord wrapped around the unit. A survey sent to all students living on campus at the time (approximately 1,300) uncovered a total of about 30 students who needed or wanted the use of a provided phone. One, I recall, was using it as a phone for his small business.

The discarded use of equipment over the past 40 years has been breathtaking. Even with the decline of computer labs, save for specialized academic facilities, the never-ending investment in hardware, software, networking, and cloud facilities grows each year. The demand for internet bandwidth is without bounds.

The conversation regarding technology has now changed. The infrastructure that dominated our planning for so many years is always being upgraded, but it is essentially accepted now as a routine cost of doing business. Admission operations rely on web-based targeting for prospective students, and geofencing is used to track those visiting campuses. Day-to-day operations are increasingly online, for everything from academic courseware to soliciting gifts from donors.

Like the emergence of higher education in the late 19th and early 20th centuries, no one planned a technology system, and no one controls the technology environment in place today. The arc of time has given rise to an organizational postsecondary enterprise now completely interlaced with an even broader and more complicated technological enterprise, neither of which is in anyone's control. As a result, the structural rigidities of conformity are expanding since it becomes too time-consuming and too costly to take novel approaches and pursue innovation. This condition reinforces the only change process available: assimilation.

Societal Norms

During my years living and working in New England, I served on 12 visiting teams for regional accreditation, mostly in that region. At the time, Charles Cook was the director of the New England Association of Schools and Colleges (now the New England Commission of Higher Education), a role he served in for many years. We interacted often, and I was in attendance at many presentations Charles offered to prepare teams of accreditors for service and to support campus-based leaders pursuing accreditation or reaccreditation. One sentence stands out most in my mind that I heard Charles utter repeatedly, "Accreditation runs on a river of form letters." For some this may have seemed like an admission of a bureaucrat running a department of motor vehicles. I interpreted it in the way I think he intended it—a reassurance that the process was well-defined, ordered, reliable, and timely. While such a process might risk a means-end reversal, wherein the process becomes the result, my experience with highly professional colleagues was a collective assurance of rigorous evaluation. The benefit was little distraction, due to logistics or process-related matters, freeing time for deeper and more evaluative thinking.

Normative patterns serve organizations well. Families benefit from routines and traditions. Institutions are served by governance and convention. Industries rely on standards and regulations to facilitate trade and expand commerce. Though less tangible, societal norms also serve citizens, as well as organizations. The strain is felt today as the societal norms adorning our social fabric are fraying. Our rhetoric has become more abrasive and our discourse less civil. The tearing effects appear across the spectrum of our interactions as the norms of the past, on which civil society has relied, are discarded.

Though most in the higher education community remain committed to the norms long established in our national enterprise, leaders interact with many individuals, particularly within our external constituencies, who are influenced by patterns of communication lacking in civility. Postsecondary institutions tend to socialize people well into the embrace of civil discourse given the historical and cultural narratives informing our shared sense of mission and values.

A term of art has emerged in recent years, which seems oxymoronic: the culture war. The unique challenge of a culture war is the weapons of choice—words and symbols. This goes to the heart of the matter for colleges and universities, as words and symbols are core to the work of educating and provide a sense of shared understanding among institutions. When these words and symbols are weaponized for use in a culture war, the academy eventually loses that which matters most: ideas. The expectation of conformity and convention may serve the academy well in seeking to generate light and not heat in a time of intensifying rhetoric. At the same time, risk comes with the immense ability of higher education to reflect the surrounding society and change through assimilation. If these corrosive effects become a contagion within institutions of higher learning, the long-term implications could be profound.

Public Policy

Public policy typically rides on a slow-moving train. I favor that mode of policy transport. In March 2020, however, public policy boarded an airline jet with the call sign "COVID-19." The speed at which adaptations occurred came too quickly to even document or communicate. On March 10, just prior to spring break that year, our senior administration at Central College had decided students would return to the campus as planned for the remainder of the semester. By March 13, we realized it would be necessary to extend spring break by a week and reconvene classes through remote access—a fundamental shift for operations in just three days. A vacuum of public policy meant that each institution, organization, and business had to assess the risk and make a choice. Guidance from public officials was conflicted, inconsistent, and unreliable. Eventually, federal, state, and local expectations and requirements were developed and still had to be reconciled due to differing opinions. It was the one occasion in which I gained an appreciation for well-formed public policy and its virtues for society. Mercifully, the journey was relatively short-lived and, remarkably, there are few if any vestiges of cobbled-together policy frameworks remaining. American society would benefit from a renewed, slow-moving train for policymaking ahead of a risk for another pandemic, but the current political dynamics do not support such deliberations.

By contrast, higher education has one of the best examples of sustained public policy in the form of federal student aid. The underlying policy principle that has served the nation well for decades is that aid follows the student. Though not without its flaws, the investment of the federal government in the education of students has proven itself worthy for generations, since the seeds were planted for this approach in the 1940s with the GI Bill. The policies have sustained bipartisan support and the programs have served the interests of individuals, institutions, local and regional economies, and by extension, the nation. It is the policy gift that keeps on giving.

In these two examples are the extremes of policymaking. One was carefully crafted well at the beginning, maintained responsibly, and deeply supported across party lines. The other was reactive given the lack of preparation despite a known risk, fraught with political conflict throughout, and abandoned by all at the conclusion.

Policymaking at the state and national level has adopted a winner-take-all mentality. Under the control of one party, a framework of laws, regulations, and rules is established, only to be undone a few years later by a change in party influence or control. The lack of sincere and responsible legislative activity leaves the executive branch to stretch the limits of its authority as the judicial branch determines what the US Congress and the US president cannot resolve on their own. The link between the erosion of societal norms and the failure of public policy is direct. Patterns of federal and state lawmaking that have direct or collateral effects on higher education are byproducts of the culture war developing over decades.

Integrating and Interpreting the Six-Pack of Change

Relying on George Keller's work as a starting point, the essential categories of his five areas for forecasting and my Six-Pack of Change remain intact. While not exhaustive, they do provide a useful framework for talking about the conditions affecting our planning as institutions of higher education. Each of the categories has relevance on its own independent of the others, but the potency is found in exploring the ways these vectors of change interact. Demographic realities affect and are affected by economic dynamics and present implications for the workforce pipeline. Advances in technology certainly affect the formal teaching and learning process, but also the pathways for informal communication. This has downstream impacts on the use of words and symbols that shape societal norms. Economic pressures drive questions about affordability, which in turn draws the interest of public policymakers in anticipating the need for a talented workforce. The best use of the Six-Pack of Change is as an interpretive vocabulary for sorting through and describing the myriad influences shaping the context in which colleges and universities operate.

For those devoting time and energy to the leadership, management, and support of postsecondary institutions, the complexity of the six-pack feels overwhelming. Yet the inherent qualities of assimilation and conformity can benefit management planning and decision-making in the maelstrom of change surrounding the enterprise. The conforming nature of higher education produces a very high level of inertia. When an institution or the entire enterprise is at rest, it tends to remain at rest. It is not easy to amass sufficient energy to initiate a broad-based process of change. A recent global pandemic is an example of the level of disruptive energy needed to overcome inertia in a short time frame. Concurrently, the process of assimilation provides a smoothing and stabilizing effect through time. Here again the experience of the COVID-19 pandemic serves as an illustration. Many changes were implemented quite quickly to adapt to an urgent condition. These changes, however, were not broadly assimilated despite predictions that the use of online and remote technologies would overtake in-person learning. It is possible, perhaps likely, that the pandemic served as an accelerant for change, but the national enterprise of higher education returned to familiar patterns of life on campus and renewed its equilibrium.

The impacts emerging in the Six-Pack of Change do appear to be intensifying as ambiguity abounds. Sudden swings in enrollment are more common as decreasing participation rates deepen already concerning population demographics. Economic impacts are more complex with higher levels of inflation, increasing interest rates, and low unemployment. Workforce expectations are moving away from the widely held assumption that an undergraduate degree is needed for long-term economic and career success. Technological development is accelerating with unpredictable consequences as artificial intelligence continues to evolve. Shifting societal norms within states or across regions are leading to political migration that may affect enrollment patterns. Public policy is being whipsawed by close elections, divided government, and an erosion of civil discourse. Political power has overtaken governance. In this maelstrom of change, there are no clear pathways for decision-making.

Levine and Van Pelt speculate on how the "the great upheaval" may unfold in the coming years. They note that, "The knowledge economy model of higher education is the end of the story, not the beginning. The first step for organizations faced with unavoidable changes in their environment is adaptation, not disruption" (Levine and Van Pelt 2021, 238). The authors rely on three examples from other industries that have been required to respond to systemic change, namely, the music industry, the film industry, and the newspaper industry. While there are clear differences among these industries and, in comparison, with higher education, they point to a common pattern of change. In each of these industries, digital technology through time imposed a different business model. They write:

> Higher education can be expected to follow a similar path. Today, the principal mode of responding to the demographic, economic, and first stage of the digital technology revolution has been by adapting. But the end game will vary for different types of institutions. *Higher education* is an umbrella term for a sprawling enterprise composed of more than four thousand, largely independently operating, colleges and universities. To say an industry will be disrupted, does not mean that all of its autonomous subunits will change in a uniform fashion. America's four thousand colleges and universities are headed for very different futures. (Levine and Van Pelt 2021, 238)

The key stakeholders invested in institutions of higher education remain committed to the survival of these thousands of colleges and universities. The outcomes, however, will vary. Some institutions will lack the depth of resources needed to manage in this changing environment and will not survive, at least not in their current form. Some with ample resources will thrive and build on the strength and momentum they amass. For most, this will be a period of ambiguity and uncertainty. These institutions will seek to organizationally adapt to changing conditions, attract and retain as many students as possible, raise all the support they can from donors, reduce operating costs in every way feasible, and find partners who align with their educational mission. One thing is certain: no institution will willingly concede.

PART II

We Learn Big Things a Little at a Time

The first part explored the dynamics of change in higher education as expressed through the arc of time by blending the unfolding of history with the development of organizational theory. The bottom line is that change in this context does not occur as many would purport or prefer. The vast, diffused, and ambiguous nature of the national enterprise changes through recursive patterns of gradual assimilation, conformity, and convention. Innovators who ignore this historical pattern are predictably frustrated by the ambiguity and organizational recalcitrance they encounter in sponsoring change. Conservers reinforce this natural tendency by using symbols, politics, and structures to amplify ambiguity and confound change. Through the course of time this loosely coupled system invariably finds a way to introduce compromise and restore equilibrium.

The focus now shifts to the application of these broad principles to the setting of the campus, in which stakeholders interact to advance the interests of individual institutions. The president (and by extension the administration), governing board, and faculty curate a collection of policies, procedures, processes, and practices through which the work of college or university is expressed. The collection is jointly held to varying degrees on individual campuses by another loosely coupled system we commonly refer to as shared governance. The next three chapters explore each of these leadership domains and the interaction of governance and management that can either clarify or cloud the collective effort.

CHAPTER 5

The Presidency Is Not a Person

I have been the beneficiary of incredibly good mentoring. More than 40 years into my career, I hear the echoes of many conversations over a period of 17 years during which I worked closely with three college and university presidents. Claire Gaudiani, then president of Connecticut College, was the first of these as I played a succession of roles in the senior administration through seven years (1993–2000). My career path then took me to an evolving experience at Northeastern University, initially under President Richard Freeland (2000–2006) and then President Joseph Aoun (2006–2010). These three mentors represented very distinct voices throughout the course of my professional development. They afforded me the privilege of seeing the reality of the presidency up close. All shared their ambitions and enthusiasms with me, but they also privately expressed their challenges and frustrations with the role. They were generous with time in sharing the intensity of the experience and pressed me to think about what I would do if placed in their circumstances. Each offered criticisms of my work, which sometimes felt harsh, but from it I drew strength as I reflected on my leadership. I owe each of them a debt I can never repay.

President Aoun served as my capstone mentor and always pushed me hard as a learner. He was aware of my openness to one day considering a presidency, and he took seriously his role in preparing me for the immense and complex task the job entails. I recall specifically two questions he asked me in my final year at Northeastern. The first presented as I was a candidate for the presidency of Central College in the fall of 2009. We sat together discussing the opportunity and he asked me, "What is your leadership going to be about?" I count this as one of the most challenging questions I have ever been asked. I had no immediate answer, and he intended the question to be rhetorical. What I realized, however, was most of my thinking had been focused on what I would "do" as a president. He was pressing me to think about who I would "be." That idea inspired a chain of thought I have continued to pursue as I still try every day to get the being question right.

The second question came just days before I completed my time in Boston. President Aoun invited me to join him for lunch. As we sat together, he noted I had worked with three presidents over an extended period of years. He then asked me, "What have you learned from each of us?" Responding to this question was helpful since it provided an opportunity for reflection that was both formative and summative. Through my response I discovered that each gave me the gift of a specific and unique perspective on the presidency; each provided examples of what can go right and what can go wrong; and each offered an array of approaches to pursuing work that is highly contextual. Though I articulated the individual contributions I derived from each mentor, the composite result of all the mentoring benefited me with a container full of useful tools that could be thoughtfully and carefully employed depending on the situation at hand. I realized the enormity of that toolbox, generously stocked by my mentors. I also realized I had just completed a 17-year internship.

No one is ready to be a college or university president. President Freeland sent me a note as I began this journey in 2010, reminding me that none of us feels prepared to embrace the fullness of the role when appointed to a presidency. His reminder was important to me at the time, but it remains true for me today. More than ever, I realize the presidency is not a person. It's an institution. My experience of relative longevity is rooted in a perspective that it takes considerable time to achieve meaningful success, as well as to prevent consequential failure. This perspective was embedded in me through the observations of my mentors, who each experienced the full measure of opportunities and challenges—some handled elegantly and some not. Whatever assessment is applied to their work with the benefit of time, President Gaudiani served Connecticut College for 13 years, President Freeland served Northeastern for 10 years, and President Aoun continues with a current total of 18 years and counting. Dedicated service for lengthy periods of time has significant benefits for an institution that boasts a century or more of history. In my case, I am the 21st president of Central College, the 8th in the last 100 years.

Even with long tenures, the service of an individual president feels constrained within the arc of time. Significant achievements that produce lasting effects rarely are manifested in terms of service less than 5 years. From experience, I would argue that 10 years is a better horizon for consequential change given the need for cycles of planning and implementation to be fully expressed. Institutions that have enjoyed generally longer presidential tenures reap the benefits of continuity and demonstrate the difference between a presidential term and the management of a presidency through time. The presidency is not a person. It's an institution within an institution.

The Churning of Presidencies

The American Council on Education (ACE) completes a periodic study on the patterns and trends associated with the college presidency. *The American College President: 2023 Edition* reports on biodemographic characteristics of presidents, along with an exploration of the career pathways that precede appointment to the role, attitudes and opinions expressed by sitting presidents, along with special topics including profiles of "Women Presidents" and "Presidents of Color" (ACE 2023).

Of note in the report is the amount of time sitting presidents have served in the position they currently hold. This is expressed as a trend reported for each edition of the periodic report dating back to 2006. The trend shows a steady decline, with an average time dropping from 8.5 years in 2006 to 5.9 years in 2022. The median is 4.5 years of service among all sectors of higher education institutions for 2022 (ACE 2023, 8, 61). The accelerating trend represents considerable turnover in presidential leadership.

During the fall of 2022, I authored two articles on the presidency, which also served to advance my interest in writing this book. "Stewarding the Presidency" (Putnam 2022b) was an opinion piece published in *Inside Higher Ed*. That was followed by a long-form article that appeared in *Trusteeship* magazine titled, "Managing the Presidency through the Arc of Time" (Putnam 2023). Here I extend that work, which began with a simple observation: the churning of colleges and university presidencies is accelerating and having a debilitating effect on our institutions.

As a matter of curiosity, I began to keep track of presidential transitions in Iowa as I witnessed colleagues coming and going at what seemed to be an accelerated rate. In 2022, excluding small, specialized institutions, Iowa was home to 29 nonprofit, public and private, four-year colleges and universities. (That number, as of 2023, was reduced to 28 with the closure of Iowa Wesleyan University.) Since I moved to Iowa in 2010, 18 of these institutions either had the same president serving or facilitated just one presidential transition. I would maintain that in each of these cases, the transitions were timely and appear to bear the earmarks of healthy continuity. Eleven of these institutions engaged in three or four transitions over a period of about a dozen years.

I have no doubt that such short-term tenures were not in anyone's plan. Nevertheless, the consequences can be profound. The pattern is destabilizing. The pace changes. Existing plans are abandoned. New plans are formed. Senior administrative leadership lacks continuity as the rapid succession of presidents invariably encourages the departures of vice presidents and deans. The cascading and collateral effects are substantive and typically run deep into the organization.

I offer no argument that all college and university presidential appointments could or should be long term. The problem is the accelerating turnover rate across the postsecondary landscape is simply breeding more turnover. When an institution becomes accustomed to frequent presidential transitions, it becomes increasingly difficult to take the appointment seriously given the repeated pattern of change. Inevitably, the commitment to sustained leadership erodes across constituent groups. Breaking that cycle of instability is an enormous task.

Institutions with sustained presidential leadership for 10 or more years tangibly benefit from the capacity to undertake and succeed with long-term, large-scale initiatives. Presidential knowledge runs deep, relationships developed across constituencies remain intact, and confidence in pursuing change is reassured. Long-serving presidents are more likely to calm turbulent waters. Rarely do they lack energy for the tasks at hand, and they remain enthusiastic about the work ahead. Those angling toward retirement are thoughtful about timing and provide ample notice in service of a smooth transition.

A different pattern is presented by presidential colleagues who have come to office following multiple transitions in less-than-ideal conditions. Most new presidents are well prepared, creative, and energetic. Some, however, buckle beneath the weight of conflicting constituent expectations. Processing and metabolizing the flow of negative energy makes it difficult to find a leadership voice in this new context. Most feel the need to react rather than respond. The tyranny of the urgent appears overwhelming. Too many are forced to look over their shoulders rather than toward the horizon. Despite the best intentions, support from the campus community and board feels tentative and conditional. In these settings, the chain of leadership continuity has been broken to the point that institutional energy moves sideways rather than forward. Disrupting this pattern is an enormous undertaking for a new president and can only be achieved with the eager commitment of the governing board. While the advantages of presidential continuity may be self-evident, the pathway may not be visible to those who must travel it.

Adopting the view that the presidency is an institution involves a change in perspective. The role is mischaracterized when the appointment of a president is viewed as the presidency. They are not at all the same. The role is inherently intergenerational. Incoming presidents collect an inheritance, embrace it for what it represents, and seek to leave a worthy legacy for successors. When this perspective is adopted, the presidency is well aligned with the arc of time and the institution can settle in for the long haul. This approach enables a campus community to tackle major challenges and opportunities that may take years to address.

An institutional view of the presidency changes the language from "my presidency" to "the presidency," perhaps even "our presidency." At its best, the management of the presidency is a team sport. It changes the question, "What does the president want to do?" to "How will the presidency respond?" A mindset shift of this kind is profoundly impactful for the governing board and the senior administration. A presidency understood to be a collective responsibility does not compromise any authority the president may need to exercise. In fact, the exercise of presidential "authority" is rarely used if it is to be effective at all. In my case, I am the chief executive officer, the chair of the faculty, and an ex officio, voting member of our Board of Trustees. Within these concurrent roles, my most important task is moderation. Influence is far more effective than authority in leading an organized anarchy (Cohen and March 1974). The inherently ambiguous nature of colleges and universities, as outlined in chapter 3, calls us to stewardship, not ownership. A single president cannot manage through the arc of time, but a presidency can if the symbols and narratives of the institution are celebrated. Change management seen through the work of the presidency receives the inheritance and leaves a legacy. More importantly, it builds capacity in the organization to protect that which matters most and to achieve the ambitions within the institution's reach. Presidents are set in place for a period of years within the wider context of a presidency. The task is to work for the eventual successors.

The view of the presidency as a collective interest acknowledges there are foundational elements long established within the institution that have been crafted over generations. Some elements will be nearly impossible to change, while other aspects can be more accommodating. Depending on the challenge or opportunity presented, the variable is time. It simply takes longer to change things more firmly established in a setting like a cathedral. The assimilation process, modeled by the Borg, reminds us that institutions, like the national higher education enterprise, experience recursive processes of innovation, conformity, and compliance. The effective presidency anticipates this pattern and seeks to facilitate it carefully. The lessons of Cohen and March (1974) in accepting the resident ambiguities and managing in the organized anarchy are helpful. Just as we have seen in canal building, the condition into which planning and organization is pursued must take into consideration the realities of the organizational terrain to be encountered. Organizational theory is a friend to the presidency.

This perspective, when embraced by the incumbent and with the support of administrative, faculty, and board leaders, fosters an environment in which a shared sense of purpose supports stability in the midst of necessary and important change. This is not an argument to be passive. To the contrary, it is a call to be active in providing an honest assessment of the presenting conditions and to set in motion plans that will advance the interests of the institution without compromising the stability on which the change management must rest. To echo earlier advice, this is about energy management within the organization, in an environment where inertia remains high and salience remains low. All this takes time and continuity. The churning of the presidency disrupts effective patterns of change. Leadership transitions have a cascading effect on people as plans are repeatedly supplanted by the next iteration, and the narratives supporting institutional development become garbled. The presidency should be managed intentionally and transparently. It is a collective work managed through time.

Patterns of Presidential Success and Failure

As noted above, not all presidencies can or should be long term. There are occasions in which a personal or professional misstep, or an unanticipated set of events, can initiate an unexpected and untimely transition. Trachtenberg, Kauver, and Bogue (2013), in their book *Presidencies Derailed: Why University Leaders Fail and How to Prevent It*, outline a set of categories to describe the types of conditions that lead to a premature departure for a president. The authors explore six derailment themes, which include the following:

1. Ethical lapses
2. Poor interpersonal skills
3. Inability to lead key constituencies
4. Difficulty adapting
5. Failure to meet business objectives
6. Board shortcomings

The book's important contribution is a collection of stories that illustrate the patterns manifested in each of these categories of derailment. Even more, the authors provide important advice about the ways in which these circumstances can be prevented by ensuring the effective preparation of the search process, paying close attention to board dynamics, and identifying and maintaining awareness of the risks. Board leaders and search committees would benefit from the practical advice offered (Trachtenberg et al., 2013).

Reaching back further in the literature is *How Academic Leadership Works: Understanding Success and Failure in the College Presidency* (Birnbaum 1992). Robert Birnbaum builds on the themes presented in the prequel, *How Colleges Work* (1988), by exploring the dynamics of the presidency more specifically. The book is rich with theoretical insight and interpretive frameworks for understanding the leadership of the president. It nests well with organizational theorists referenced earlier in this writing, including Cohen and March, as well as Bolman and Deal. Birnbaum also relies, in part, on a study of leadership in higher education, referred to as the Institutional Leadership Project (ILP), an in-depth five-year research effort intended to explore the work of college presidents and other academic leaders.

At the conceptual base of Birnbaum's theories undergirding academic leadership were a set of myths about the work of presidents. The composite view of the myths is that constituents often seek a president who is characterized as having a vision, serving as a transformational leader, possessing charisma, maintaining professional distance, and presenting a pleasing array of styles and traits (Birnbaum 1992, 24–38). These characteristics, however, are nuanced and easily misinterpreted.

Candidates for presidencies often are asked to describe their vision for the institution they are seeking to serve. Those asking the question are presumably more interested in asking, "What are you planning to do to us?" The notion of vision is best understood symbolically, especially in view of the ambiguities present in an organization. The president plays the role of interpreting, articulating, repeating, and animating the vision born of broad-based understanding of institutional history, culture, and ambition. The president is not the sole author of a vision, but they are the most important narrator and curator.

Charisma is a complex characteristic since it must be understood in context. Birnbaum describes this as a two-edged sword. A capacity for meeting the public well and inspiring confidence is a strong attribute, but such abilities are undermined if there is little substance evident in the work through time. Authenticity and sincerity can serve as a counterbalance for charisma alone, but clarity and consistency of performance are essential to center presidential leadership for the long term. I have known many college and university presidents, and there are few I would characterize as personally charismatic. Most would trade respect for their stewardship of the presidency, and affirmation of professional competence, for the fleeting rewards attributed to a charismatic personality.

There are reasons to maintain some level of professional distance, but the assertion by some that the president should remain more or less hidden and work through others is misguided. Here again there is a balance to maintain. Birnbaum noted in class that "interaction creates likability and likability creates trust." Depending on the size of an institution, the availability of the president is an important factor in building community and maintaining influence. During my early days as a college president, my family and I felt like we were under constant surveillance in our local community. Over time that feeling receded as people became acquainted with us and the novelty of a new president in town gradually wore off. Humanizing the presidency, however, is an important task for serving effectively in the role. Early attempts to lobby me for the sake of self-interest gradually turned to less-pointed questions like "How is your family?" The presidency naturally evolves, and managing professional relationships is a part of that evolution. I have been required to make very tough personnel decisions, especially where some form of misconduct was present. That duty can never bend to the weight of a personal relationship. It is possible, however, to remain cordial and respectful in virtually every situation.

Many in college and university communities admire an individual viewed as a transformational leader. This descriptor is held in contrast to a transactional leader. Birnbaum (1992) refers to the transactional leader as being associated with maintaining the status quo, while the transformational leader is seen as introducing new ideas and new forms. This is a false dichotomy since effective leadership requires a balancing and rebalancing of both qualities. Reaching for the transformational requires the stabilities associated with the transactional. Managing through the arc of time involves periods in which the president must be generative and press forward an agenda for change. There are also periods when consolidating gains requires the day-to-day work of management and is equally worthy.

The management styles and personality traits of presidents vary widely, and Birnbaum suggests there is little evidence these leadership characteristics are of material importance in the success or failure of a leader. Still, the identified personal traits and perceived management style of a candidate have an outsized influence in presidential searches. It is often the dominant issue for candidates and search committees since it is the most obvious and accessible category of assessment. It takes discipline to avoid this as a narrow line of inquiry and expand the evaluation to matters more substantive.

From time to time, I am contacted by a professional colleague interested in pursuing a career as a college or university president. In some cases, the individual is active in a search, while others are simply seeking to validate their aspiration. In either case, I always suggest a two-step approach. A candidate quickly becomes emotionally invested in a search, so it helps to begin the process with a disciplined and dispassionate analysis designed to clarify readiness to undertake the responsibilities demanded. In assessing an opportunity, the first step is to establish intellectual distance from the role and approach it as an analyst or consultant would do. This is an attempt to answer the question, "What is necessary for *any* candidate to be successful in this role?" I encourage them to take time to write out their assessment. The second question is, "What is necessary for *me* to be successful in this role?" The exercise provides an opportunity to determine if the advice they would give to a colleague is advice they would accept for themselves. The essential issue is one of alignment between the candidate and the potential assignment.

As noted above, conventional wisdom would tell us that the composite image of these five characteristics results in a successful president who has vision, is charismatic, maintains distance, is transformational, and possesses the styles and traits desired. This framework is based entirely on the individual president, not the presidency. Using the same characteristics, the view from the presidency would reframe the interpretation of these qualities with a set of questions. Will this individual:

Have the capacity to interpret, articulate, and champion our shared vision?

Inspire and animate that shared vision?

Establish and maintain professional integrity in
relationships?

Animate this institution to pursue new ambitions, while
assuring operational excellence?

Manage in a way that aligns well with the culture of this
organization?

Setting the president in the context of the presidency, whether
in selection or evaluation, assesses the work of the individual
president during the period of appointment with the needs and
interests of the presidency.

The factors that lead to derailment and the myths that sponsor oversimplified views of the presidency are notes of caution
as candidates contemplate opportunities and as search committees and boards assess candidacies. There is a deeper conceptual
framework, however, that goes beyond the unfortunate missteps
and misalignments that may lead to an early departure for a sitting president.

Birnbaum describes in detail three archetypal presidencies:
the *modal presidency*, the *failed presidency*, and the *exemplary presidency*. These presidential pathways are not strictly associated
with years of service, though the length of service would seem
to correlate. A failed presidency would tend to be shorter and an
exemplary presidency longer, with the modal presidency more
likely somewhere in the middle. The text is rich with interpretation as each type of presidency is explored and the three are
thoughtfully compared and contrasted (Birnbaum 1992).

The *modal presidency* is what one would expect to be average.
The key element in distinguishing this path is that the president
begins with support across all major constituencies, including
the board, administration, and faculty. Birnbaum writes,

Initial successes and the withholding of criticisms lead modal presidents to become more certain of themselves, to overestimate their effectiveness, to become less sensitive to complaints, and to diminish two-way communications. During the honeymoon period, presidents can do little wrong; constituents who support a president's actions are quick to say so, and any who are troubled are apt to watch and wait rather than speak up. But all too soon, new presidents are no longer "new." Constituents become less likely to give the president the benefit of the doubt, or to excuse presidential judgments with which they disagree on the grounds that the president is not yet familiar with the campus. The press of routine obligations, as well as the need to attend to the sporadic crises of institutional life, make it difficult for presidents to continue to engage in the processes of interaction and discussion that marked the first phases of their terms. (Birnbaum 1992, 90)

Of particular note for the modal presidency is the characteristic erosion of support from the faculty. Birnbaum writes,

Presidents who initially communicated with faculty in order to make sense of institutional life now feel less need to do so. They are more willing to develop, and have more confidence in, their interpretations based on their increasing experience. As faculty criticism develops, it may be discounted by modal presidents as coming from unrepresentative cabals or stoically accepted as reflecting an unfortunate but inescapable consequence of firm leadership. (Birnbaum 1992, 90)

The fundamental characteristic that defines the modal presidency is the nature of the communication with faculty. Increased criticism can lead to decreased interaction and eventually to misunderstanding and miscommunication. How this quite common circumstance is handled determines the ultimate profile of the presidency. The horizon of leadership may be diminished depending on how the core constituents manage this condition. The characteristics of a modal presidency may lead to either a failed presidency or an exemplary presidency depending on the circumstances and any attempts made to intervene. In the end, the modal pathway may result in a presidential departure not considered to be premature. In fact, if these conditions persist too long, then some constituents may simply assert the president just stayed too long. Waning faculty support is common in presidential tenures, but the eventual outcome depends on the interpretation of the circumstances and the interim measures applied to improve communication and facilitate interaction. The manifested characteristics of a modal presidency may or may not be the end of the story.

The *failure* of a presidency is typically damaging to the institution. The extent of that damage depends on the cascading and collateral effects manifested across the organization.

> Failed presidencies begin like modal presidencies, but end with the president not only losing the confidence of the faculty, like the modal president, but also the confidence of the board or of administrative colleagues or even of both. (Birnbaum 1992, 94)

Whether precipitated rapidly by a single event (perhaps the mismanagement of a crisis or some form of misconduct) or a more gradual series of actions incrementally accelerating toward a downward spiral, the failed presidency tends to end abruptly. There is also some additional risk if the appointment of the president was not widely supported or if the process of selection was viewed as illegitimate. Here again the work of Trachtenberg et al. (2013) cited earlier delves deeply into this pathway.

Exemplary presidents begin with general support across constituencies and are able to maintain sufficient support among faculty members to endure. Birnbaum describes the journey as follows:

> Exemplary presidents enter office with high faculty support, which they cultivate and preserve primarily by maintaining, even as they mature in office, the enthusiasm, institutional commitment and desire to interact with faculty that typify new presidents. Exemplary presidents are seen as both competent and as sensitive to the social and political dynamics of their institutions. They not only make good decisions but follow good processes. . . .
>
> The most important characteristic of exemplary presidents is that they are seen as continuing to respond to the faculty and willing to open themselves to faculty influence. They listen to faculty, and they support existing faculty governance mechanisms. While modal presidents are likely to treat communications and interaction as instrumental devices which become less important once they have learned about the campus, exemplary presidents are more likely to view them as essential and continuing components of evolving communities. The modal president sees communication as a means to an end; the exemplary president sees it as an end in itself. (Birnbaum 1992, 98)

The study Birnbaum undertook included a validation step for the pathways presented by examining the work of old presidents through a retrospective analysis. The results largely confirm the pathways presented as reasonable frameworks for interpreting presidential service. The findings associated with old presidents added a dimension of importance in thinking about the work of managing through the arc of time. Birnbaum (1992) noted that "old presidents who followed the exemplary path were more likely than the other two types to be cognitively complex and therefore able to interpret institutional life through multiple perspectives" (100). Related findings indicated exemplary presidents were less likely to use *adaptive* strategy (changing what you do) and more likely to use *interpretive* strategy (changing how you think). They tended to see leadership as a "process of social exchange, based on reciprocity and mutual influence" (101). There was evidence of a commitment to shared governance. Emphasis was placed on seeing the institution as a collective enterprise in which the day-to-day work was inseparable from a "concern for people and process" (101).

These archetypes aid thinking about the success of an individual presidential appointment but more importantly about the patterns of success witnessed across the life of the presidency as an institution within an institution. It stands to reason that exemplary presidents lead to healthy presidencies through time. A modal president may do no harm to the institution of the presidency but is also less likely to leave an important and influential legacy. The failed president is typically detrimental to the presidency, a situation made worse if the presidency experiences a series of failed presidents. Great care should be taken to restore the presidency when debilitated to this extent, but it is not an easy task since confidence erodes quickly and disaffection takes hold. The cycle can be hard to break, but collective work among stakeholders can be effective if sustained through an extended period of time.

Stewarding the Presidency

The presidency of an institution viewed through the arc of time is composed of a series of presidential appointments—many successful, some not. It is interesting to read the advertisement and prospectus for a position open today. They follow a consistent pattern. Most of the content is designed to promote the institution and boast of its achievements and admired features. Some space is dedicated to describing the mission of the college or university, reporting its scope of programs, services, and activities. A somewhat smaller section outlines the qualities and qualifications expected for the successful candidate. The least amount of space is devoted to the challenges and opportunities anticipated, in which the challenges are actually cast as opportunities. Little, if any, of the content is related to a thoughtful articulation of the inheritance available in the presidency, the stewardship expected of the presidency, and the hoped-for legacy of the presidency. There's typically a "to do" list, but unlikely a "to be" list.

As a student of my own practice, I have observed a pattern in my experience I also see in others. At some point in the second or third year, the pushback comes. Often a new plan is developed, campaign activities are set in motion, administrative transitions have been implemented, and things are beginning to change. In my case, I experienced pushback from some trustees, some administrators, and some faculty. It was not an overwhelming challenge to my leadership, but it became clear that the honeymoon was over. By experiencing that change in attitude and behavior around me, I became aware there are inevitable vulnerabilities in executive leadership. I have seen presidential colleagues faced with the same pressures I experienced become confrontational in an attempt to demonstrate strong leadership. The escalating conflict resulted in an early departure. Likewise, I have known colleagues who made a mistake serious enough to raise fundamental concerns about their leadership. They quickly moved on. Others were not well suited for the role as the performance pressure mounted. Suddenly, a new professional journey began. These examples fit the profile of the failed presidency, though I will admit for many of them the word "failure" seems too harsh. Most were well-intended and worked hard. I can empathize, however, as I reflect on the early challenges I encountered, realizing if I made some bad choices along the way, that could have been me.

I also feel a connection to the modal presidency. Between years seven and nine in my appointment, the rough and tumble of shared governance intensified to a point that the administration, faculty, and board were all engaged in a season of tension sufficient to test the structures of governance and strain relations. At the time this situation surfaced, I reread Birnbaum's work on the presidency. At that point I felt like the modal presidency would be my pathway. Going back to my organizational theory guides, however, I rediscovered the Cohen and March themes about ambiguity and the methods for leading in an organized anarchy. I followed the advice: persist, spend time, facilitate the opposition, and so on. I flipped the frames offered by Bolman and Deal to explore options in the structural, symbolic, human resource, and political approaches to advancing the organization. These tools and methods provided the intellectual platform I needed to sustain my leadership through a more challenging season.

I would not presume to evaluate my work as a president in the context of the 170-year presidency at Central College. I am far enough along that absent a very serious misstep, it is unlikely my service would be considered a failure. I think some see my path as modal, despite the fact that my tenure is now well beyond a decade. My aim is to be exemplary and so I work to that end with benefit of age, and hopefully some accumulated wisdom. Part of this has been the realization that the presidency is a trust to which I must be faithful if I am to honor the work of my predecessors and advantage the work of my successors. More than ever, I am determined to not overly bind that future even as societal change accelerates around me. More flexibility rather than less has been a thematic influence in my more recent work. At the same time, there are elements that need to be more stable and secure to ensure a strong foundation on which they can continue to build. I am increasingly persuaded that continuity in the presidency begins with understanding it as an institution within an institution and treating it as such. But I cannot do the work alone.

Stewarding the presidency necessarily begins with the governing board. The board is uniquely positioned to ensure the presidency is perceived as more than the service of the current occupant. Reinforcing that perspective in the minds of constituents and nurturing the processes of governance, leadership, and management that will undergird the collective responsibility for the future is the board's enduring work to manage through the arc of time as a community of trust.

CHAPTER 6

A Community of Trust

Even a casual observer of the US Congress would acknowledge a loss of community in both the US Senate and the US House of Representatives. Stories are told of days in which the bridges of personal relationship could withstand the weight of political disagreements. The common interpretation is divided government, reflecting a divided nation, is the root cause of the dysfunctions manifested today. I would argue it's not the divided opinion at the core of the problem, but a fracturing of governance, which has had devastating impacts on community, resulting in an erosion of trust.

It would seem intuitive that governance begins with community. Humans gather in service of a common interest and then organize to achieve expressed aims. That is, of course, a pattern evident throughout human history. Established communities, however, rely on principles of interaction to maintain healthy organizations since people come and go and participation in any community is fluid through time. The systems that undergird enduring communities take the form of governance. Community may be the starting point, but alone it lacks staying power. Accordingly, there is a reciprocal quality present as community gives rise to governance and governance is the means by which communities are sustained.

Returning to the US Congress, repeated transgressions of governing norms have a corrosive effect. If governing rules, conventions, and practices are traduced too often, then community erodes as trust is gradually compromised. In recent years, our nation witnessed rules broken, conventions manipulated, and norms compromised through the exercise of political brute force. Both major political parties now routinely engage in such practices. The cascading and collateral effects are profoundly negative as one infraction leads to another and opposing sides escalate the conflict. The damage to governance produces a decline in trust, which, in turn, harms community. A sense of community within federal, state, and local governments is increasingly rare. The culture of expectations no longer views the systems of governance as sacrosanct. If a narrow political purpose is served, then governance is seen as expendable. This pattern comes with great societal cost.

College and university governing boards are subject to the same dynamics. The healthy development of a board necessarily involves the building of a unique community through shared narratives, vocabulary, and experiences often expressed through oral tradition. Concurrently, devotion to consistent governing principles and practices advances the work of the board and reinforces community as it honors the established patterns of interaction that build trust.

The culture of institutional governance is informed by the interplay between the formalities of the governing process and the informalities of relationship building. This returns us to a theme explored earlier, "interaction creates likability and liability creates trust." The methods for maintaining balance take many forms. The exact approach is less important than the shared understanding that emerges from the consistent application of the patterns through time. A sustained, well-organized, and intentional effort is necessary to foster an environment in which community and governance dance together on a floor of trust. Spending time dancing together in this way may seem frivolous to some, but it is an investment that pays huge dividends through the arc of time.

A Peculiar Dance

As a candidate for the presidency of Central College in 2009, I reviewed a considerable amount of information about the institution while preparing for the interview process. Through the course of my reading, I noted in the college bylaws the existence of a special category: trusteeship. The bylaws state:

> ARTICLE II, Section 9. A special form of non-voting trustee membership shall be provided for faculty and student representation such that each would have an equal number of trustees. The committee on trusteeship will review each year the slates presented by the faculty and students, recommending candidates for election to the board. The faculty trustees will serve a two-year term and the student trustees will serve a one-year term, both commencing on July 1. Special trustees shall be accorded all privileges on the floor but will not be eligible to vote. (Central College Bylaws)

I contacted the consultant supporting the search about this provision. He was a retired college president, with many years of experience in the role. I was interested in learning what he knew about the faculty and student trustees and how these roles functioned. To my surprise, I discovered there were five faculty trustees and five student trustees. The size of the board's voting membership is permitted to range from 18 to 40 (typically 35 to 40), so this was impressive participation of faculty and student members actively and consistently present to the work of the board. He indicated to me this was unusual given his observation and experience in the profession, but by all accounts, it seemed to work well in this setting.

While I was aware some institutions appoint or elect a single member of the faculty and/or a single student to serve as a trustee (in some cases with voting privileges), I had never seen anything quite like this. Even more remarkable, the board appointed the 10 special trustees to several of the standing board committees. This was a long-standing practice at the college. During the interview process it was never a topic of conversation, though I remained incredibly curious about how this functioned.

Here's how it works. In each cycle of election, processes unique to the faculty and student body are engaged. In the case of the faculty, the process is tied to committee elections with some provisions for representation of major faculty committees, as well as expectations for disciplinary representation. The process takes the form of approval balloting recording the preference of the faculty for those deemed suitable to serve. The slate of candidates is then forwarded to the board's committee on trusteeship. Unless there is an interest or concern within the committee related to the composition of the slate (a very rare occurrence), those receiving the highest vote totals are presented to the board for election to a two-year term on an alternating year basis. There are no specific term limits.

The students use a different approach. Student trustee applications are gathered. The student leadership, including the sitting student trustees, engage in a formal review process of the candidates and then recommend a slate to the committee on trusteeship. This process is more akin to a self-perpetuating approach. The students are elected to a one-year term, though they are eligible for reelection during the period of their enrollment. The administration provides any needed support for the processes but plays no formal evaluative role. Since I am a member of the committee on trusteeship, I have the opportunity to express a concern about a candidate if I feel compelled, but I have never done so.

The faculty and student trustees participate in plenary sessions of the board, but they are excluded from executive sessions. The same is true for committees. Faculty and student trustees are appointed to the academic excellence committee, enrollment committee, and student experience committee. One faculty member is also appointed to the finance committee. In addition, the faculty and student trustees submit written reports to the board on any topics they deem appropriate. During the formal business session of the board, faculty trustees give an oral report or presentation, as do the student trustees. Both the faculty and student trustees have direct access to the board chair, and typically the faculty trustees meet with the board chair in advance of an upcoming meeting to review any items of interest.

When I describe this design of governance to presidential colleagues, they are uniformly bewildered. I rehearse this unusual governance structure not to advocate that others adopt it. In fact, I sometimes describe Central College as higher education's version of the Galapagos Islands—there are species of things here that don't exist anywhere else in the world. As a case study, however, the example is helpful in conceptualizing a community of trust.

Seen through the arc of time there is something powerful in this model, despite the risks inherent in broad participation. The board chair when I was hired was Dave Wesselink ('64). His grandfather, John Wesselink, served as president of Central College from 1925 to 1934. By the time Dave retired from the board as an emeritus chair and trustee, he served 31 years. At the time he was a student, the provision for student trustees was not yet in place. Dave was succeeded by Lanny Little ('74), a trustee for more than 35 years, with service as board chair for 7 years and now chair of the committee on trusteeship as the elder statesman. The provision for faculty and student trustees was added during his senior year. Lanny and a fellow student served as the first student trustees, in the 1973–74 academic year. Now in his sixth year as chair, Tej Dhawan ('91) has served as a trustee for more than 20 years. He also served as a student trustee, as well as student body president, during the 1990–91 academic year. It is no surprise current student trustees often remark that one day they hope to return to the board as a voting member.

The continuity extends to faculty trustees as well. Tej's academic advisor when he was a student was Robert Franks, now an emeritus professor. Robert served as a faculty trustee for several terms during his long career as a faculty member, right alongside his former student, Tej. Faculty members who have served in this role have first-hand knowledge of how the board works through its committees, how the board processes information and deliberates, and how dedicated board members are to the well-being of the college. This adds value to deliberations within faculty governance since the practices of the board of trustees are known to current and former faculty trustees who understand how the board functions.

The Board of Trustees at Central College has two other characteristics that are less common among colleges and universities. First, there are no term limits for service as a trustee. The committee on trusteeship maintains a thorough self-evaluation and trusteeship committee evaluation process as members complete terms and are considered for reelection. This includes surveys, giving patterns and attendance records, as well as a qualitative evaluation regarding the quality of service provided to the board. The long tenures noted above among our most recent chairs are not necessarily uniform across the board. It is far more common for board members today to serve two to four terms of four years, thus a length of service between 8 and 16 years. Overall, there is a healthy pattern of board turnover. Second, 90% of current board members are alumni of the college. Critics of this model could point to the risk of insularity. That is a fair concern and one to be carefully monitored in this design. What counterbalances that risk is the healthy culture of the board, coupled with its disciplined practice of governance. It is a socially rich and intellectually rigorous setting—a good example for a community of trust. In this context, identifying quality candidates to the board takes on a different form. The best candidates for trusteeship are obvious. They are already behaving like effective trustees before they are ever appointed.

A Governing Community

A community of trust is nurtured through many years and is highly contextual within a particular institutional setting. The example I provided of Central College has emerged over at least the last 50 years. Through those decades, changes occurred. Articles of Incorporation and Bylaws have been rewritten, policies and procedures updated, and practices evolved as needed. Technology drove some of these changes. Best practices have been identified and incorporated. Through all this, however, the stability of governance has not been compromised since this is a recursive and incremental process of assimilation. The duties of the governing board go beyond just its ministerial functions. It is the duty of the board to also embody the ideals of community through its lived experience, and thereby preserve the collective trust for future generations.

The Association of Governing Boards of Universities and Colleges (AGB) offers a well of published resources and professional conferences on the principles of trusteeship, duties of care, board functions and practices, and many related areas. I commend the various publications and events available to those interested in trusteeship. Having participated in two AGB conferences designed for joint participation of sitting institutional board chairs and presidents, I have benefited from the advice and counsel offered through these sessions. Attending as a team of two provides opportunities to participate in plenary sessions, but also to have extended periods of time to meet privately as a team. It's a luxury of time well spent.

The takeaway from the experience is there are broad patterns associated with governing boards and trusteeship that inform conventions and drive some degree of conformity across the higher education enterprise. The standardization of practice is robust. Board cultures, however, are unique. This is evident in the presentations of experts on trusteeship, but even more in the discussions among participants as they explore the commonalities and contrasts across institutions. Some boards are very businesslike and maintain personal distance. While they may be unfailingly cordial, the time spent is focused on ministerial duties. Others are more highly relational and devote considerable time to social interaction as well as business. Building a community of trust does not depend on style, however. In either example, the presence of reliable governance ensures the best interests of the institution will be served. My own board is very social, but they are equally committed to rigorous deliberations and disciplined action. Another board charged with leading a public institution, for example, may have a very different social dynamic but can still build a community of trust relying on good governance. It's easy to see where things can go wrong. A board with high levels of social engagement can erode a community of trust if cronyism or nepotism in some way compromises reliable governance. Likewise, a board with lower levels of social engagement can risk trust by not knowing colleagues around the table. The duties of the board are well established, but the cultural dynamics of a collective are fluid as membership changes over time. Curating a board as a collective is a task of discernment. This is the group that must embrace the arc of time more than any other.

When Things Go Wrong: The Tyranny of the Urgent

It is said that the half-life of a doctoral dissertation is five years. Mine is now 30 years old, but I have been revisiting it recently since the circumstances I see today seem to rhyme with that era in higher education history. As noted in chapter 4, the baby bust that followed the baby boom reached its demographic nadir in 1994, just as I was completing my research. I was interested in the unfolding effects demographic decline and economic pressure were yielding on campuses across the country. In time, the focus of my work centered on trustees as I studied institutions facing an existential threat. The title of the study was "The Role of Formal and Informal Sources of Information in Trustee Decision-Making at Small Private Colleges Struggling for Survival" (Putnam 1994).

My initial idea was that the closure of a college should be predictable by data analysis. To some extent that is true. More recent analysis offered by Robert Zemsky, Susan Shaman, and Susan Campbell Baldridge, in *The College Stress Test* (2020), makes a strong case that certain profiles represented in institutional data point to a higher risk for failure. However, the simple fact that an institution presents a high-risk profile evidenced in data analysis is not sufficient to predict the actions a governing board will take. An actual decision for closure, merger, or reorganization is a very complicated process of discernment. This is certainly informed by data but also by many competing and confusing sources of information. While decisions with such consequence likely involve emotion, for some institutions this can become the overriding aspect of decision-making. The idea of a closure or merger seems unthinkable. The process of decision-making when boards were faced with a crisis was the focus of my study.

Though I reviewed the crisis situations of a dozen or more institutions, I narrowed my study to three. One of the colleges closed during the period of my research. Another merged into a larger nearby university. The final institution was attempting to reorganize and remained hopeful in its efforts to survive as an independent institution. Subsequent to my research, it was eventually acquired by a university in its region. The design of the study was a multiple case study approach utilizing both quantitative and qualitative analysis through a triangulated design relying on (1) extant data and information provided by each institution in the form of reports, presentations, and minutes to their governing boards; (2) a survey of trustees regarding their use of information in decision-making; and (3) interviews with several trustees from each college. The intent was to explore the sources and uses of data and information when the decisions at hand were highly consequential.

Among the findings of the study was a realization that seemingly objective information was often viewed subjectively by members of the governing board. Under normal conditions, trustees tended to be deferential to each other and the administration in processing information. Absent some obvious stress, there was a broad acceptance of the status quo. At the extreme, this can be viewed as a benevolent indifference. Heightened scrutiny emerged when matters grew to be sufficiently complicated, but by that time these boards were often chasing the crisis, rather than managing it. The tyranny of the urgent surfaced. Trends and patterns missed along the way might have served as an early warning. Board members blended formal and informal sources of information available to them. There were consistent attempts to validate one source by the use of another. Through the process at each institution, the community of trust was placed under considerable stress. The narratives outlined a journey through years of deliberations, marked by periods of hope and despair. Though the emergence of a crisis in some cases seemed to appear quite suddenly, these were stories typically told over a decade if the roots were adequately traced. When the threshold of viability was crossed, the community of trust was tested in decision-making that was daunting, as well as urgent. Depending on the culture within the governing board, this was for some very personal—for others, very corporate. The common characteristics of board member reflections were various manifestations of ambiguity. There were varying viewpoints about how the situation evolved, concerns about the reliability of the formal information provided, myriad uses of informal information, and questions about who could be trusted.

The sources and uses of formal and informal information varied widely as reported by respondents. The general pattern revealed was a practice of trustees receiving and digesting the formal information provided but seeking to validate it through many different informal channels. One trustee described this approach as follows:

> It's a combination. I wouldn't make a decision without one or the other and I think often times the formal is first for me, but the informal is critical. Because so often in the formal presentation you'll get just what is on the surface and its through informal conversations and digging and really probing around that you find out what's really going on. (Putnam 1994, 181)

Weighing the information from all sources was a highly subjective process of integration and filtration. One respondent described it like this:

> Take all the different sources and weigh them according to where they were coming from. . . . I had to listen to certain constituencies such as alumnae, past chairs, [and] faculty. With each of them I had more information than any one group. I had to weigh what was personal dislike, from fact. Rumor had to be weeded out. Some things couldn't be substantiated. . . . I'd love to have a formula, but a judgement [sic] must be made. (Putnam 1994, 184)

The practice of assembling information and processing it in order to form an opinion on a matter before the board immediately drew attention to the level of confidence a trustee could reach given the information obtained and reviewed. As the crisis evolved and pressure mounted to make decisions, board members struggled to assign credibility to the information they received, reinforcing the desire to pursue independent verification of what they believed to be reliable. Commonly reported by several respondents was a view that the confidence they had in a presenter would determine for them the reliability of the information they were receiving. Board members offered many comments consistent with this interpretive task. Three respondents in particular captured the sentiment as follows:

I'd use the word reliability rather than trust, because I didn't mistrust anyone. But, I had some questions as to whether the information that was provided was correct. Not that it was intentionally falsified, but whether you are looking at the numbers correctly and analyzing it correctly. Personal history is also a factor. We all deal with life this way. When you say something to me, my first question to myself is, "who is saying this," as opposed to "what is he saying."

You must go back to the source to see if information was reliable. A written report while it might be a formal presentation, if it shows bias, is no more reliable than an objective observer.

It obviously has to do with the individual. If it's a person that I have enormous respect for, then obviously it's going to weigh the equation differently. But if it's a person I've been given reason to believe is not doing the very best job, then I've got to not only look at the surface of what they are saying, but then try to figure out beyond that. (Putnam 1994, 153, 183–84)

The survey results for the study indicated 90.1% of the 59 respondents across all three institutions agreed that they judged the quality of the information they received in light of the confidence they had in the person presenting the information (Putnam 1994, 206).

With some insights regarding the sources and uses of formal and informal information, as well as the confidence trustees expressed about the information they received, the dynamics of board decision-making were also explored in the study. Myriad factors entered into the deliberations beyond the specific details gathered through formal and informal channels. Some spoke of a paralysis in decision-making processes, often informed by emotional interactions. One respondent noted, "The decision was made with a sense of determination and desperation—determination to keep the school open, and desperation that we didn't know how to do it" (Putnam 1994, 186).

The process itself was agonizing for trustees faced with such an intimidating set of circumstances. They expressed frustration with the unreliability of information, leading to increasing levels of uncertainty and inaction. The reflections of four trustees summarize the dynamics of decision-making set in this stressful condition:

> Real but unpleasant information was not presented to the board members early enough to change the outcome. Local leaders with significant roles on the board, but relatively short history with the institution were prime movers in a period of significant economic decline for the whole region/state. . . . I still believe we acted both too quickly and too late without sufficient consideration of the alternatives. . . .
>
> We talked probably for a year before, that unless something happened significantly, we had to merge or close. And then the

question is when do you have to make that decision. . . . I think
we recognized that we had this very small window in which we
had to come to a conclusion. So I think you might argue that
we should have done something six or eight months before, but
the problem with doing that is that it becomes the board taking
over the management. . . . Once it became apparent that management could not [turn things around] then the board had to
step in.

I think the administration failed to anticipate the impact of
declining demographics and a poor economy. Also, they failed to
recognize and react to early warning signs. The board was also
behind, but largely has to rely on input from the administration.
Had we moved sooner, we might have postponed the final result,
but I doubt it would have changed it. . . . Our information systems
were too crude and the staff stretched too thin to provide the data
needed. People did the best they could.

It just seemed impossible that the Lord would let [the college]
fail. And when we got to the point where we said, we can't go on
any longer, we were just sort of surprised. There had been so
many miracles in the history of [the] college that we expected
another one. (Putnam 1994, 119, 151, 157–58)

The decision-making process, regardless of the sources and
uses of formal and informal information, and the confidence expressed about the information available, was further complicated by the presence or involvement of internal and external
stakeholders, in some cases laced with emotion about the downstream impacts that would cascade from a decision or its sense
of mission and purpose. One quote in particular summarized the
interplay of formal and informal sources of information in
decision-making:

I felt well informed about the realities of the crisis and knew about it soon enough, even though some information was missing, distorted or incomplete, because the crisis was about whether the administration was accurately conveying to the Board the status of the faculty, student, and campus situation or masking the reality. The resulting battle for the attention of the institution caused personal observation, personal confidence and accurate information to be clouded by faulty interpretation and stilted reporting at formal meetings by reporters who feared reprisals from other factions present at meetings. Although I was prepared to formulate an opinion, I always knew what a report would say before I read it because of its source and because of outside discussions before I received it. And, since most community members were fed disinformation from both sides, I spent a lot of time on this crisis. (Putnam 1994, 189)

Admittedly, the stories of these institutions in distress represent extreme cases, though 30 years later similar conditions are again pressing institutions, both public and private. As explored in chapter 4, declining demographics and economic pressures, among other external threats, are common. These high-stress situations test the capacity of a board to operate as a community of trust. They reveal the underlying patterns of governance, the disciplines of decision-making, and the extent to which board development has prepared a board to manage well when the decision-making stakes are high. At its best a community of trust develops the organizational muscle strong enough to be steadfast in tough times. The likelihood that a board will perform well under difficult conditions is diminished when there has been little investment in board education and development.

Evident in the research were patterns that complicated the work of the boards during these days of stress and anxiety. The sources and uses of information of all types had a confounding effect. Buffeted by waves of conflicting data, constituent lobbying, relational breakdown, and feelings of inadequacy and uncertainty can have a paralyzing effect on a board. In each case, the situation became more fluid and unpredictable. The well-trodden pathways of governance during better times were abandoned for novel activities and abrupt interventions that only served to destabilize the situation further. Inertia engaged and ambiguity expanded as the anarchy of organization intensified. The presenting conditions were, in the end, too much to overcome, but some of the trustees wondered if they had known earlier in the process, could they have made better or different decisions. It is possible that no interventions would have worked, even if timely. The unfortunate outcome, however, was accompanied by relational breakdown, growing mistrust, depletion of assets, and organizational dysfunction. These past stories are a harbinger of potential risks for the present day.

Obvious in the comments offered by the trustees in the study were concerning reports of administrators shaping information or even falsifying information. As I spent time reviewing standard internal and external institutional reports and presentations, I discovered a few occasions in which the information given to the board was inconsistent and inaccurate. The integrity of administrators was a persistent theme with trustees. Some interpreted these discrepancies as mistakes or simply noted the information was incorrect. Others believed they had been deliberately misled. Whatever the case, the community of trust necessarily extends to the administrators of an institution, most notably the president.

Since completing the study, I have maintained that a core responsibility of the administration of a college or university is enabling effective board decision-making. Some reduce this to transparency, and such a commitment is the bedrock. The responsibility the administration has to the board is to provide a comprehensive and unvarnished view into the condition set presented without manipulation. This practice involves consistent reporting, clear definitions, insightful analysis, and good counsel, with an ongoing commitment to board education and development. The task of the administration is to help the board to learn with sufficient depth of understanding to inform sound decisions. Integrity demands the trade-offs of decisions be clearly understood. The profile of risk should be explored. The contours and nuances of a given situation should be made plain. A community of trust is supported by a high level of interdependence among all who are present to its work. A culture of relational integrity is wedded with a commitment to governing integrity. This means that members of the trust community don't cut corners.

The relevant policies, procedures, processes, and practices require unfailing devotion. That may be easy when drifting through calm waters, but if the disciplines of governance and the deepening of healthy relationships is not pursued when it is easy, it is unrealistic to believe they can be relied on when the waves crash. Just as we practice emergency procedures in many aspects of our lives to promote public safety and preparation for when tragedy strikes, a community of trust must rehearse its ways of being and ways of doing over and over again to maintain discipline and focus on the task at hand. These are immensely important skill sets for institutional leaders and worth all the time and energy they require.

Getting Things Right through the Arc of Time

A governing board, as a community of trust, maintains a constant awareness of the arc of time. The strength of the institution they lead is found in the enduring presence built through decades, if not centuries. Change occurs through gradual assimilation set in the context of a national higher education enterprise in which innovation is processed collectively through a recursive pattern of conformity and convention. Building a future requires a commitment to creating the essential conditions for healthy change to be introduced and managed to success.

Fostering a community of trust in the arc of time must be intentional. In the case of independent colleges and universities, most utilize a self-perpetuating model for succession. Public colleges and universities typically use a different model of appointment or election. Either approach can create the means for thoughtful onboarding and succession planning to maximize durability of plans designed and set in motion through time. Careful attention to this is essential. As members are socialized into the life of the board, learn its cultural patterns, and embrace its ambitions, the narrative of the community is internalized. Welcoming new trustees should be far more than an orientation to function and process. It should be a passing on of a shared story intended to ensure stability even in the midst of change. When facing challenging times, a knowledge of institutional history and long-term potential opportunity becomes essential in stretching thought to reach beyond the next quarter, semester, or academic year. A board characterized by fits and starts, but little patience with the unfolding of time, will likely be ineffective.

Many decisions undertaken by a board are necessarily set on a long horizon of planning. The most obvious are buildings and infrastructure that come with a term of decades. Less obvious, but equally important, are decisions to award tenure to members of the faculty who may be serving on a campus for a career lasting decades. The management of an endowment is a trust held collectively that lasts into perpetuity. The decision to take on long-term debt is a decades-long commitment taken on behalf of future board members. The development of an academic program from the earliest days of consideration and planning to full implementation with successful graduates could take 5, perhaps even 10 years. I often remind the trustees I serve with that my job as president is to focus on the eighth graders since I have 5 years to think about where they will be when it comes time to join our campus. It is the role of the board, however, to focus on 8-year-olds who are 10 years away from their college experience.

A community of trust manages the immediate without getting caught in the tyranny of the urgent. It anticipates emerging challenges, because it is not afraid to talk openly about demographic challenges, economic uncertainties, workforce expectations, technological innovations, societal change, and public policy. Trust within a community of governance looks hard for where trouble may come from and seeks to be prepared as situations unfold. The trustees I surveyed and interviewed more than 30 years ago from institutions that no longer exist shared one sentiment more than any other: "We got on this too late." Trustees who are students of their practice are devoted to active learning, not passive attendance. A presiding board is a passive board. A meddling board is a distracted board. An engaged board is a learning community focused on the long-term horizon and prepared to offer advice and counsel to the president, and act in accordance with its governing mandate. It exercises its duties of care with sobriety. It builds relationships that foster trust. Through the arc of time the community of trust instills within the institution a respect for history, a value for disciplined governance, and a commitment to horizon thinking. Modeling this temperament is one of the most important gifts a board can give to the institution it serves. It sets a tone for the integrated work of management and governance because we are in this together.

CHAPTER 7

We're in This Together

Governance is the nexus between tradition and innovation. It reinforces tradition by extending the time horizon of accepted institutional patterns and norms. Through deliberation and codification, the structures of governance support process legitimacy and promote broad acceptance for decisions made. The benefit is organizational stability; tradition is honored and rehearsed. Governance is also the processor and validator of innovation. Fresh initiatives undertaken by an institution may be generated through an ad hoc process but will, in time, be presented to formal governance channels for consideration and adoption. Governance serves as the repository for past innovations and defines the accepted roles, responsibilities, and rules for future change management. Accordingly, governance is a point of integration. It allows time for the cultural symbols and political influences associated with an innovation to be processed effectively by the organization.

Some view governance as the enemy of innovation and attempt to circumvent, marginalize, or overpower the established processes. A dependency on governance can be uncomfortable for innovators, who may interpret the organizational systems as a diversion or distraction, in addition to providing aid and comfort to traditionalists. When properly organized, however, governance can be an ally to innovation. If an innovation cannot withstand the test of governance, then it is unlikely to succeed when facing real-time organizational dynamics within an institution. In that sense, it's a proving ground.

For those who feel burdened by governance, I suggest governance is like a cathedral—it is built to endure through time over generations. This is a virtue. Most innovators intend their novel ideas to have staying power. Yesterday's innovators often become tomorrow's traditionalists. Governance is also like the Borg, as assimilation is how institutions of higher education metabolize innovation and gradually integrate new ideas with traditional practices. Interpretive and adaptive change are both at work here. Governance is like canal building in which the characteristics of organizational terrain matter considerably; innovators seek favorable conditions for launching initiatives. The integration of tradition and innovation is a shared responsibility organized through shared systems and processed through shared governance. Working effectively within a model of shared governance takes time, but it is time well spent.

Share and Share Alike

One of the few documents with an enduring presence in higher education emerged in 1966 through the coordinating efforts of the American Association of University Professors (AAUP) in collaboration with the American Council on Education (ACE) and the Association of Governing Boards of Universities and Colleges

(AGB). The *Statement on Government of Colleges and Universities* was "jointly formulated" by the three associations, which in turn, endorsed the document and commended it to their members. Early in my career this document was commonly referred to as "the joint statement," a term I will use throughout this chapter. It resides today on the AAUP website 57 years after its release, having been updated in 1990 to remove gender-specific references. Despite criticism that the statement did little to address the means by which institutions could practically employ shared governance at a variety of institutional types across the country, the statement has served as a source for some key shared governing principles. The introduction to the document notes the following:

> The statement that follows is directed to governing board members, administrators, faculty members, students, and other persons in the belief that the colleges and universities of the United States have reached a stage calling for appropriately shared responsibility and cooperative action among the components of the academic institution. The statement is intended to foster constructive joint thought and action, both within the institutional structure and in protection of its integrity against improper intrusions.
>
> It is not intended that the statement serve as a blueprint for governance on a specific campus or as a manual for the regulation of controversy among the components of an academic institution, although it is to be hoped that the principles asserted will lead to the correction of existing weaknesses and assist in the establishment of sound structures and procedures. The statement does not attempt to cover relations with those outside agencies that increasingly are controlling the resources and influencing the

patterns of education in our institutions of higher learning: for example, the United States government, state legislatures, state commissions, interstate associations or compacts, and other interinstitutional arrangements. However, it is hoped that the statement will be helpful to these agencies in their consideration of educational matters. (AAUP 1966)

This statement of "mutual understanding" outlines principles for governance that allow for contextual interpretation in a wide variety of institutional settings—public and private, small and large. The core principle is an acknowledgment of a primary role played by a particular constituent group within the governing framework, with full attention to the duty that internal governing body may bear. The attitude is one of stewardship, not ownership, with due respect for the legal, regulatory, and fiduciary responsibilities that must be upheld across an institution. In all cases, the key element is communication. The document states:

Joint effort in an academic institution will take a variety of forms appropriate to the kinds of situations encountered. In some instances, an initial exploration or recommendation will be made by the president with consideration by the faculty at a later stage; in other instances, a first and essentially definitive recommendation will be made by the faculty, subject to the endorsement of the president and the governing board. In still others, a substantive contribution can be made when student leaders are responsibly involved in the process. Although the variety of such approaches may be wide, at least two general conclusions regarding joint effort seem clearly warranted: (1) important areas of action involve at one time or another the initiating capacity and decision-making participation of all the institutional components, and (2) differences in the weight of each voice, from one point to the next, should be determined by reference to the responsibility of each component for the particular matter at hand, as developed hereinafter. (AAUP 1966)

Through the years, I have been interested in various assertions made by colleague trustees, faculty, and administrators about how this widely held concept of shared governance is expressed in practice. The joint statement does a good job of setting the essential parameters, but there is still plenty of room for interpretation. Therein lies the challenge. This arena of governing interaction can be further complicated given the posture taken by any of the three principal players in shared governance. For example, overbearing boards risk undermining the delegation of responsibility they defined for the faculty and administration. Such actions create confusion and turmoil. The old saying for governing boards is "nose in, fingers out." Likewise, a president who oversteps in the work of faculty or interferes with the duties of the board can risk generating more heat than light across the organization. The role of the president in supporting the work of the faculty and board requires diplomacy. It does not diminish the authority that may need to be exercised if conditions warrant, but as the joint statement suggests an adverse action on a matter delegated to the faculty should only be taken "under exceptional circumstances" and "clearly communicated" (AAUP 1966). Likewise, the president has an affirmative obligation to not only inform and advise the board but also to ensure its governing prerogatives are honored.

To explore the dynamics of shared governance in practice, I begin with the faculty. I do so because most business organizations define the roles and responsibilities of board governance and management. Unique to the higher education setting is the role of the faculty in the context of a professional bureaucracy—one in which the expertise of the faculty is highly relevant to the governing of the institution.

Which Faculty Are We Talking About?

A faculty member at an institution I served indicated his interpretation of shared governance boiled down to the "share" of governance a faculty is entitled to hold. For example, it was his view that if the president of the college had an interest in appointing a college-wide committee to address a college-wide interest, the faculty should determine independently of the president how the faculty will be represented on that committee in a manner binding on the president. This would include the number of participants, as well as their selection. Extending the concept, it was clear in his comments that the faculty members appointed or elected by the faculty would serve as a caucus of delegates. This would obligate them to return to the faculty as a whole in order to receive feedback or instruction on any position representatives would take on behalf of the faculty.

In another example, a faculty colleague once indicated to me that shared governance in his view would stipulate individual members of the faculty be present to specific financial decisions. When I asked how he would see that happening in practice, he offered the following example. "Let's say the college received an unrestricted bequest of $500,000. I should be at the table when the decision is made to allocate those funds." Both examples represent the desire of some faculty members to extend their individual and/or group governing authority beyond policies and procedures related to education, to further include any matter of interest or concern to the institution.

The joint statement outlines the role of faculty from a different vantage point:

The faculty has primary responsibility for such fundamental areas as curriculum, subject matter and methods of instruction, research, faculty status, and those aspects of student life which relate to the educational process. On these matters the power of review or final decision lodged in the governing board or delegated by it to the president should be exercised adversely only in exceptional circumstances, and for reasons communicated to the faculty. It is desirable that the faculty should, following such communication, have opportunity for further consideration and further transmittal of its views to the president or board. Budgets, personnel limitations, the time element, and the policies of other groups, bodies, and agencies having jurisdiction over the institution may set limits to realization of faculty advice. (AAUP 1966)

Of note in the described faculty role is the primacy expressed within the framework of governance on matters attending to the teaching and learning process, and faculty status (i.e., tenure and promotion). In this arena of institutional activity, the governing board delegates to the faculty the stewardship of these educational matters and remains deferential to the professional judgment of the faculty within this aspect of the institution's mission. Having delegated the responsibility to the faculty, however, the faculty also adopts a duty of care under the supervision of the governing board, which is entitled to ensure the scope of the educational enterprise fits within the resource base available and is consistent with the institution's mission. The role of the president (and by extension the administration) is to facilitate this interaction and ensure the processes outlined are followed and requisite information to support decision-making is available. The presidency is the connecting point between the respective governing roles prescribed for the board and faculty. For the most part this is routine, as matters being transmitted from the faculty to the board are typically ministerial. There are occasions, however, when controversies emerge within the faculty as a governing body, within the board as a governing body, or between the two. When resources are scarce, the intensity of interaction can be amplified. In such cases, the president often takes on a role less executive in tone, adopting a more diplomatic voice.

Part of the challenge in understanding and interpreting the role of faculty is a distinction between the faculty as a teaching body made up of individuals members, and the faculty as a governing body, which operates as a collective. This has been a long-standing source of confusion and occasional controversy. A particular example serves but requires a bit of background to establish its relevance.

Through time, the AAUP has authored statements on the principles of academic freedom and tenure. The original statement was crafted in 1915. In 1925, ACE convened a conference intended to shorten the statement. This resulted in a revised document endorsed by AAUP, ACE, and the Association of American Colleges and Universities (AAC&U). This statement was further considered during a joint meeting of the AAUP and AAC&U in 1940. While the statement was not changed, interpretive comments were added. This body of work continues to evolve with the times, but it has reliably informed institutional policies related to academic freedom and tenure for more than a century and has been a great service to the academy. I reference this work not to draw attention to the specific issues of academic freedom and tenure, however. Contained within the statement is the following sentence: "College and university teachers are citizens, members of a learned profession, and officers of an educational institution" (AAUP 1940).

From time to time, I have heard faculty members reference this sentence in asserting that individual members of the faculty are "officers" of the institution, even the corporation. One such interpretation I have heard is that a college or university should be viewed as a bicameral form of government, with one chamber in the form of the governing board and the other in the form of the faculty. Accordingly, the assertion is made that the president should be subject to both chambers. Consequently, the president would in this model report to the faculty as well as the governing board. Taken to its logical conclusion, independent authority would exist for the two chambers, and a matter before the institution would be considered by the faculty and the governing board separately. Each would adopt legislation then reconciled through a process of negotiation in conference or in joint session. The resulting joint action would then be delegated to the president to implement and administer. Though it was never the intent of the AAUP in using the term "officers" to assign authority, it is an interesting perspective to contemplate. While such a role for faculty has never existed in American higher education, there are faculty members who view this level of authority as an idealized version of faculty governance.

The actual context for the use of the term "officer" by the AAUP statement on academic freedom and tenure, however, does not reference any authority ascribed to members of the faculty. It refers to a responsibility. The relevant section of the document states the following:

College and university teachers are citizens, members of a learned profession, and officers of an educational institution. When they speak or write as citizens, they should be free from institutional censorship or discipline, but their special position in the community imposes special obligations. As scholars and educational officers, they should remember that the public may judge their profession and their institution by their utterances. Hence they should at all times be accurate, should exercise appropriate restraint, should show respect for the opinions of others, and should make every effort to indicate that they are not speaking for the institution. (AAUP 1940)

As "educational officers," members of the faculty are described as having a responsibility to uphold a duty of care, knowing that public statements they offer may also be attributed to the institution they serve. The statement does not, however, ascribe to them the roles, responsibilities, or duties associated with a corporate or institutional officer.

Returning to governance, it is worth remembering the ambiguities inherent in an organized anarchy, particularly with the use of the term "faculty," which may be used to describe an individual, a group, or a governing body. Members of the faculty, individually and collectively, will seek to assert as much autonomy and authority as they can while avoiding as much accountability and responsibility as possible. This is not an indictment. It is simply the reality of organizational dynamics in which shared governance is created by the decision of a governing board to delegate specifically defined matters, associated with the practice of education, to those with the expertise in the profession of education. That delegated role, however, is set within the context of an institution. The full scope of institutional responsibilities certainly includes those educational interests, but they also go beyond those interests as scarce resources, competing demands, and regulatory matters impinge on the degrees of freedom available. These conditions give rise to the political dynamics of choice in which the aforementioned ambiguities of purpose, power, experience, and success are intertwined (Cohen and March 1974).

Institutions with unionized faculties have an added dimension of consideration as collective bargaining interests need to be defined and reconciled within the framework of shared governance. In this model, the power bases shift depending on the issue at hand and may impact the mechanisms of governance utilized. Defining the boundary conditions becomes the essential element in maintaining clarity on the processes engaged. The joint statement is agnostic about the presence of a union for faculty. The essential principles of shared governance remain. The document notes the following:

> Agencies for faculty participation in the government of the college or university should be established at each level where faculty responsibility is present. An agency should exist for the presentation of the views of the whole faculty. The structure and procedures for faculty participation should be designed, approved, and established by joint action of the components of the institution. Faculty representatives should be selected by the faculty according to procedures determined by the faculty. (AAUP 1966)

The strength of the joint statement is its commonsense approach. The pattern of thought expressed throughout is that communication is the centerpiece of shared governance. Communication is facilitated by an organizational design with well-articulated procedures and practices, and clearly defined roles and responsibilities. The stability of the underlying systems of governance is the bedrock of trust, as outlined in the concept of a community of trust framed in chapter 6.

The creation of the faculty as a formal governing body with specific delegated duties for which it is primarily responsible, coupled with a meaningful participatory role in which the faculty has sufficient information to express its voice, is the foundation for shared governance. Such an approach does not eliminate the risk of controversy, but it provides the organizational pathways by which controversies are addressed, conflicts are managed, and decisions are made. An institutional commitment to shared governance is crafted and maintained by the governing board.

The Board's Decision to Share Governance

Most governing boards I have encountered through my career have a love-hate relationship with shared governance. They are socialized into an enterprise that has long valued the distribution of responsibility and love the sense of engagement it represents. Many carry very high levels of respect for faculty members, especially if they are alumni of the institution they serve. They hate it because it's messy, time-consuming, and occasionally annoying. The joint statement was crafted in a way that accommodates all types of colleges and universities. Accordingly, the particular style of shared governance adopted by an institution is unique to its setting. For some institutions, shared governance is held in high esteem, while at others it is viewed with disdain. Sponsoring broad participation involves risk. How a board interprets and manages that risk determines the temperament of, and tolerance for, shared governance. The joint statement offers the following observations regarding governing boards:

The governing board of an institution of higher education in the United States operates, with few exceptions, as the final institutional authority. . . . Since the membership of the board may embrace both individual and collective competence of recognized weight, its advice or help may be sought through established channels by other components of the academic community. The governing board of an institution of higher education, while maintaining a general overview, entrusts the conduct of administration to the administrative officers—the president and the deans—and the conduct of teaching and research to the faculty. The board should undertake appropriate self-limitation. (AAUP 1966)

The key to understanding the role of a governing board in the context of shared governance is that it never gives away its authority. In the case of my own institution, the bylaws of the college outline clearly the reserve powers of the board; the delegated roles and responsibilities of the president, the faculty, and the student body; and the affirmation that all matters before the college are subject to its review and approval. A corporate resolution is adopted at least annually specifying the few individuals authorized to sign a contract or otherwise obligate the institution to perform in a specified manner. For most institutions, this would be a uniform practice.

A counterexample surfaced during a conversation I had with a presidential colleague relatively new to the role. This individual asked a question about who on my campus was authorized to sign a contract. I rehearsed the list of officers endowed with such authority. My colleague then indicated that on her campus almost anyone could sign a contract. Whether the discipline of signature authority had devolved at that institution over time, or adequate provision for signature discipline had never been established, it represented a dissipation of governing board authority even beyond a reasonable scope of management control all the way to individual agency.

The board is the author of shared governance and must take the role seriously through time. Fluid participation as administrators and faculty come and go, even with long tenures, reveals the risk that a long-established governing practice can atrophy if not well documented and enforced. Shared governance requires strict discipline for it to be well maintained and durable over the years. Educating board members on the principles and apparatus of shared governance is a crucial responsibility.

When properly conceived, defined, and executed, shared governance offers many rewards. A healthy model encourages investment in the work of the institution. The arc of time benefits immensely from solid governance as many ambitions take years to design and implement. The disciplines of governance provide a sturdy platform for multiyear efforts in which decisions are processed broadly, and plans set in motion are understood to be long-term efforts. Disruptions also have a place to go in which the policies and procedures of governance undergird decision-making when urgent matters are present. Maintaining the structures of governance is critically important despite the mundane sense of routine sometimes experienced. When a crisis hits, the reliability of that structure will be tested. Servicing it along the way with preventive maintenance is time and energy well spent. That certainly involves the work of board leaders, but it also is a key responsibility of the president.

The Responsibility of the Presidency to Facilitate Shared Governance

The role of president is mostly associated with the authority delegated by the governing board to an individual. In my case, the bylaws of Central College describe the role as follows:

> The president shall be the college's chief executive officer and the chief adviser to and executive agent of the board of trustees. His or her authority is vested through the board of trustees and includes responsibilities for all college educational and managerial affairs. The president is responsible for leading the college, implementing all board policies, keeping the board informed on appropriate matters, consulting with the board in a timely manner on matters appropriate to its policymaking and fiduciary functions, and serving as the college's key spokesperson. He or she has the authority to execute all documents on behalf of the college and the board of trustees consistent with board policies and the best interests of the college. (Central College Bylaws)

While the emphasis of this statement is on executive authority, also resident in the text is an obligation to advise, inform, and consult. The range of potential topics is vast, but included is the important role the president plays in advising, informing, and consulting on matters of governance. This is a reminder that the presidency is not a person. The president is endowed with a span of authority carefully measured and always subject to the board. The *presidency*, however, is far more important. If the governing board is the author of shared governance, then the presidency is the narrator. Governance is a system, but it is also a story. It's a story about how things get done. Preserving the norms and honoring the practices of governance is an essential function of the presidency. The predictability of the process matters. The patterns of interaction should remain consistent. The presidency facilitates governance in consultation and collaboration with board leadership. In this respect, the presidency is the steward of the process serving governance as defined by the board. The joint statement offers the following:

> The president shares responsibility for the definition and attainment of goals, for administrative action, and for operating the communications system that links the components of the academic community. The president represents the institution to its many publics. The president's leadership role is supported by delegated authority from the board and faculty.
>
> The president must at times, with or without support, infuse new life into a department; relatedly, the president may at times be required, working within the concept of tenure, to solve problems of obsolescence. The president will necessarily utilize the judgments of the faculty but may also, in the interest of academic standards, seek outside evaluations by scholars of acknowledged competence.
>
> (AAUP 1966)

The various roles of the president are specified here. The aspects of authority and influence are both represented. Of note, however, is the reference to "operating the communications system that links the components of the academic community." This is about governance and the work of the presidency in supporting it. The presidency is uniquely positioned in the system of governance to advise, to offer an opinion, to point to the rules and conventions, and to be a resource for facilitating process. It keeps records and documents decisions. The presidency includes the president's staff, board professionals, and senior administrators who collectively support the work of the governing bodies. It's a system that organizes and orchestrates the work of governance.

Shared governance as a system is a complex process requiring a lot of time and energy to sustain. Adding to the complexity is the frequent intersection of governance and management, another point of reconciliation in an organized anarchy.

The Ambiguities of Governance and Management

Though the broad principles outlined in the joint statement have benefits for describing the ideals of shared governance, there remains enormous confusion about how the behaviors of governance and management are to be exhibited by governing boards, faculties, and administrators, within a framework of shared governance. The root of the ambiguity is the notion of primacy or the expectation of one having a defined primary role. It is a short distance from primacy to authority in such an ambiguous setting. For example, the joint statement contemplates the primacy of the faculty in matters related to the teaching and learning process. The primacy delegated does not set aside the de jure authority of the governing board, but it does give rise to a de facto assumption that the actions and recommendations of the faculty should be honored except in "exceptional circumstances," a term not defined. As a practical matter, most legislation adopted by a faculty has been vetted by the administration, given the attending needs for financial, physical, and human resources. A healthy system of governance begins with open channels of communication and ample advance notice that a matter is under consideration. That said, controversial issues can easily move in the direction of conflict if differing views invoke questions of authority. In routine circumstances there is generally a commonly held attitude of stewardship and responsibility. When disagreements or disputes arise, that attitude can quickly change to a more direct assertion of ownership and authority.

Shared governance as contemplated in the joint statement is highly contextual. Accordingly, the structures and processes of shared governance should be well-defined and articulated, utilized consistently, and maintained carefully. These become the foundation for dealing with novel conditions when presented—typically without warning. The patterns of governance learned through time, the predictable behaviors modeled by key players, and the reliable skill sets strengthened by regular use make it possible to adapt existing processes in a manner that does not undermine the overall governance structure. When the pressure is on, there is an instinct among some to start a new process to address the emergent issue. This is usually a bad choice. Using and adapting the existing structures of governance utilizes familiar patterns. It may be that a routine agenda for a governing group is set aside to deal with a more immediate concern, but that is a relatively minor adjustment compared to redefining structures, processes, roles, and responsibilities.

Governance has limitations. It can be effectively applied to agenda setting, policymaking, ministerial decision-making, and the like. It is, however, a poor substitute for management. Too often colleges and universities use governance models to undertake the work of management because it appears to symbolically soften perceptions of authority. At the same time, those engaged in governance risk stepping into management because it is so tempting to bind the prerogatives of management through policymaking.

As a manager, I take seriously my role in supporting the governing work of the board and the faculty, but I do not operate the presidency in a model of governance. I do not rely on a cabinet structure; I use an executive management team model. The team is composed of my direct reports, and our purpose is management. As a working group, we are project focused and task oriented. We are data driven and evidence based in our planning and decision-making. While I retain the authority assigned to the president, we endeavor to manage the presidency together. We do not emulate the patterns of governance. There are no votes cast and no minutes taken, though we do carefully track projects. We support the work of governance in every way possible and remain deferential to the governing roles and responsibilities assigned to others. Governance and management can and should be complementary, but one cannot be the substitute for the other. They are two different organizational disciplines. There is a unique role for the presidency to play in integrating governance and management through executive leadership. The presidency is the steward of governance, providing diplomacy, narration, and procedural guidance. Those leading faculty and board governance often rely on the presidency to ensure things are done properly. It is a ministerial function the presidency is best positioned to play.

Governance and management seen through the arc of time require an enduring commitment across generations of trustees, faculty members, and administrators. The inheritance is richer when the disciplines of governance and management have been administered well. The documentation of the past is more than institutional history. Devotion to the structures and processes of governance are a living legacy for our successors. Leaders learn from those who stewarded these activities before them, remain devoted to the principles of shared governance supported by sound management, and pass on what is learned for future generations.

PART III

The Illusion of Control

I sometimes offer a word of advice to family, friends, and colleagues: *Don't be the victim of other people's choices.* In plenty of circumstances this advice can't prevent an unfortunate situation, though I maintain it is worth trying. The real benefit is found in gaining an awareness of when a choice by another may be impactful and when interpreting the potential consequences may have explanatory value. Observing the cascading and collateral effects of a choice can also inform pattern recognition as future conditions surface.

Those who play individual or collective leadership roles in higher education soon realize that many of the circumstances encountered are associated with limited degrees of freedom to act. There are boundaries set in place by the legal, regulatory, or policymaking authorities surrounding and pervading institutions. The marketplace for students drives expectations for performance that quickly become compulsory if an institution is to be competitive. The perceptions and perspectives of constituents and stakeholders in the enterprise bind us to conformity with long-standing patterns. At the same time, the future may demand adaptations that amend or supplant these interests. The dynamics of interaction and engagement with those who seek to influence the enterprise are too numerous to count, but collectively, they produce complexity and constrain progress.

CHAPTER 8

Who Is the Learner and What Should They Learn?

Our vice president for athletics, Eric Van Kley, tells the story of a conversation he had with three of our students a few years ago. He asked them, "Why did you choose to come to Central College?" After looking at each other (as if they were thinking, "Should we really tell him?"), they recounted the events leading up to their collective college decision. These students knew they wanted to enroll together, but they were torn between attending Central College and another nearby institution in Iowa, Simpson College. As they struggled with the decision, they realized Central and Simpson had an upcoming football game on the schedule. They decided they would enroll at the college that won the game. Central won. Stories like this terrify enrollment managers.

Administrators and faculty typically think of students as part of the campus community and, therefore, an inside constituency. During the events associated with our commencement season, I thank students for the many contributions they've made to their shared experience and note the indelible impression they've left on the campus community. Students, by way of their participation, shape their own experiences and set the stage for those who follow. So, in this way they are internal stakeholders. Students are also subject to institutional supervision in the conduct of their course of study, as well as some behavioral expectations consistent with the nature or category of enrollment (i.e., resident, commuter, undergraduate, athlete, employee). They often play a role in governance through various governing structures made available to them. Some are involved in the management of various programs, services, and activities essential to the work of the campus.

Students are also participants in two external marketplaces—one on entry and one on departure. As "paying customers," they are consumers in the marketplace for higher education, considering options for their undergraduate experience. Further, they are eventually graduates of our institutions in labor and/or graduate/professional school markets. The multifaceted role they play in the college and university setting makes the relationship rich with ambiguity. Notions of control, therefore, are contingent on the context in which any particular interaction takes place as students are consumers, participants, and eventual graduates.

Maintaining enrollment through this complex web of roles and responsibilities is a tall order. Those who study the dynamics of student retention offer the reminder that institutions are always marketing to enrolled students. Many students have mobility in the marketplace and continue validating or searching for the educational experience they desire, if not sufficiently satisfied. Through the lens of a policymaker, administrator, faculty member, trustee, or parent, decisions made by a student are—or should be—informed by careful analysis and reflection on the strengths and weaknesses of a given institution. Those of us who lead colleges and universities with predominantly traditional-age students like to think of them as rational actors; but as noted above, a college choice for an 18-year-old can be somewhat random. For more mature students, life is often complicated by the competing demands of family and professional life, making the durability of a college choice subject to many outside factors. Regardless of age, a change in an intimate relationship, an illness or injury, a disagreeable roommate, the lack of playing time on a team, a job change, or an unhealthy lifestyle are just as likely to lead to a change in direction as a decision driven by a rational choice for a new major toward an emerging professional interest. The journey of human development is complicated because the years of late adolescence and young adulthood are predictably uncertain. Things can get messy. Life tends to get in the way.

The Learner

Set in this intensely ambiguous and fluid notion of "student" is a deeper inquiry into the concept of "learner." The title for this chapter poses two interrelated questions about the nature of the learner and what should be learned. There are no agreed-upon answers. The attending ambiguities are vast, practically limitless. In this sense, the learner is the "needle" and the body of knowledge the "haystack." Locating this process in a single institution is an intimidating task. Nevertheless, the higher education enterprise must continually find a way to cope with the ambiguity. Successful learning is, in part, dependent on the quantity and quality of prior learning, developed capacities for engaged learning, and motivation to reach for further learning. Accordingly, the process of teaching and learning is as varied as it is complex.

There is, however, one fundamental characteristic at the core of connecting a learner to a teacher. It's about relationship.

James Garfield served as president of the United States for a brief period in 1881. He had a notable career as a politician, having served nine terms in the US House of Representatives. Within months of his election as president, he was shot by Charles Guiteau, a disillusioned supporter disappointed by not receiving the recognition he believed he deserved. Though Garfield initially survived the gunshot wound, the resulting complications eventually took his life.

Garfield came from modest roots in Ohio, and his educational journey eventually took him to Williams College in the 1850s (Miller Center 2023). At Williams he encountered Mark Hopkins, who served as president from 1836 to 1872. Years later, though the legendary story has variations, Garfield, in paying tribute to Hopkins, noted the ideal college was Mark Hopkins on one end of a log and a student on the other. Regardless of how the story actually unfolded, the image remains deeply engrained in the psyche of American higher education. Learning is, by its nature, relational. It is fundamentally a human enterprise in which learned individuals devote themselves to teaching students. It's the "other end of the log" that matters.

Through the arc of time, the nature of that relationship has evolved as the technologies of learning advanced gradually by assimilation decade after decade. Yet a craving remains in most students to know and be known by those who teach them. Whenever I ask friends and colleagues about their best learning experience, it invariably involves a teacher, described in terms of relationship. Parker Palmer, in his book *To Know as We Are Known: A Spirituality of Education* (1983), notes the following:

Practicing obedience to truth in the classroom, practicing responsive listening between teacher, students and subject, is not finally a matter of technique. It depends ultimately on a teacher who has a living relationship with the subject at hand, who invites students into that relationship as full partners. Here is the largest hospitality of a teacher who has a fruitful friendship with the subject and who wants students to benefit from that relationship as well.

Students will often say that their favorite teachers are ones who are enthusiastic about their subjects even if they are not masters of teaching technique. More is happening here than the simple contagion of enthusiasm. Such teachers overcome the students' fear of meeting the stranger, this subject, by revealing the friendship that binds subject and teacher. Students are affirmed by the fact that this teacher wants them to know and be known by this valued friend in the context of a well-established love. (Palmer 1983, 103–4)

Some argue Palmer's notions of teaching and learning are quaint and sentimental but hopelessly outdated. For them, such lofty ideas are meant for earlier generations, less sophisticated in the advanced technologies of instructional design. It takes too long, is labor intensive, and expensive. Yet this impulse for relational, rather and transactional, learning remains.

In 2014, Gallup completed a study, titled *Great Jobs Great Lives: The 2014 Gallup-Purdue Index Report*, in partnership with the Lumina Foundation and Purdue University. The goal of the research was to "study the relationship between the college experience and college graduates' lives" with particular attention to the level of engagement they experienced in the workplace. The study included more than 30,000 college graduates across the United States. The findings revealed the six undergraduate experiences most closely related to long-term life outcomes. They are as follows:

- I had at least one professor at [College] who excited me about learning.
- My professors at [College] cared about me as a person.
- I had a mentor who encouraged me to pursue my goals and dreams.
- I worked on a project that took a semester or more to complete.
- I had an internship or job that allowed me to apply what I was learning in the classroom.
- I was extremely active in extracurricular activities and organizations while I attended [College].

The results also reveal that at one end of the spectrum, 82% of graduates who reported having all six of these experiences during college also reported that college prepared them well for life. By contrast, those who reported having none of these six experiences indicated they were well prepared for life after college only 5% of the time. The key finding was that higher levels of engagement in mentoring relationships and experiential learning during college lead to better outcomes in life (Gallup 2014).

Intuitively, learners know the role of a teacher and the level of engagement in learning are essential elements in an educational experience we consider to be rewarding. The learner, therefore, is the primary consideration in the educational context, and to lose sight of that is to drift into a means-end reversal in which the process and content of learning is divorced from the learner. I will return to the learner later, but for now turn to the second question: "What does the learner need to learn?"

The Grand Disconnect

Two long-standing questions continue to be debated: (1) Is the purpose of education a public or private good? and (2) Is the role of education to provide liberal or vocational education? Both questions present false dichotomies. The balance between individual success and collective well-being are complementary features of a sound education.

To explore this issue, I return to the 1947 Truman Commission Report, the product of the President's Commission on Higher Education, published as *Higher Education for American Democracy*. I wrote on this topic years ago in a series of blogs titled "Education for Democracy" (Putnam, 2012) and rehearse some of that content here.

One might imagine in the wake of World War II the focus of education would be entirely on labor markets driven by the need for economic and technological advances. To the contrary, the report's foundational elements in seeking to promote democracy argues for a person-focused perspective. The report states:

The first goal in education for democracy is the full, rounded, and continuing development of the person. The discovery, training, and utilization of individual talents is of fundamental importance in a free society. To liberate and perfect the intrinsic powers of every citizen is the central purpose of democracy, and its furtherance of individual self-realization is its greatest glory. (President's Commission 1947, vol. 1, 9)

If our colleges and universities are to graduate individuals who have learned how to be free, they will have to concern themselves with the development of self-discipline and self-reliance, of ethical principles as a guide for conduct, of sensitivity to injustice and inequality, of insight into human motives and aspirations, of discriminating appreciation of a wide range of human values, of the spirit of democratic compromise and cooperation. Responsibility for the development of these personal qualities cannot be left as heretofore to some courses or a few departments or scattered extracurricular organizations; it must become a part of every phase of college life. (President's Commission 1947, vol. 1, 10)

The educational benefits for the individual, however, are balanced against the needs and interests of society. The report continues:

Higher education has always attempted to teach young people both spiritual and material values. The classroom has imparted the principle of collective responsibility for liberty—the rule that no one person's right to freedom can be maintained unless all men [and women] work together to make secure the freedom of all.

But these efforts have not always been effective. All too often the benefits of education have been sought and used for personal and private profit, to the neglect of public and social service. Yet individual freedom entails communal responsibility. The democratic way of life can endure only as private careers and social obligations are made to mesh, as personal ambition is reconciled with public responsibility. (President's Commission 1947, vol. 1, 10)

This vision for education placed before our nation was not a recipe for the creation of personal wealth. It was not a formula for national economic development. It was an assertion that a society rich with democratic values will yield shared success. Accordingly, the role of education is to facilitate the creation and dissemination of knowledge for the public good, to develop the skills needed among citizens for sustaining individual freedom and a collective well-being, and to nurture a shared experience sufficient for ensuring equality and justice.

The Truman Report also makes clear an assumption that the practicalities of learning for vocational benefits are also essential. The report states:

> Although general education, as the term is currently used, is concerned with the nonspecialized activities of living, it is by no means antagonistic to vocational education. Rightly conceived, the two are complementary. General education should contribute to vocational competence by providing the breadth of view and perspective that make the individual a more effective worker and a more intelligent member of a society of freemen.
>
> It is urgently important in American education today that the age-old distinction between education for living and education for making a living be discarded.
>
> The idea has long prevailed in our tradition, and it is still widely prevalent today, that a liberal education is one thing and a professional or vocational education is another, that the two should be sharply differentiated, that one is preparation for labor, the other for leisure.
>
> The ends of democratic education in the United States will not be adequately served until we achieve a unification of our educational objectives and processes. American education must be so organized and conducted that it will provide, at appropriate levels, proper combinations of general and special education for students of varying abilities and occupational objectives. (President's Commission 1947, vol. 1, 62–63)

The report goes on to articulate how general education and professional education should be of "equal dignity and importance" making them "interdependent." More than 75 years later, the struggle continues with these issues as policymakers, employers, students, and educators encounter the historic ambiguities surrounding the learner and what should be learned.

College and university presidents occupy a space in the middle of this debate. It is by no means a position where there is any control, though there are opportunities for influence, at least at the institutional level. The range of stakeholders explore these questions in very different ways.

I engage routinely in discussions with policymakers about two closely related topics—education and workforce. For many years, federal and state officials have been fusing the two terms to the point they are now inseparable as policy interests. The aim, of course, is clear. For society to maintain progress and benefit from economic expansion, our nation needs trained workers to fill jobs closely aligned with industry demands. As one policymaker noted for me recently, "Our universities need to be graduating students who will fill these jobs." For many policymakers, the societal domains of "education and workforce" can be more conveniently stated as "credentials and jobs."

The counternarrative among many in the academy is that while education and workforce are clearly related, conflating the two tends to be overly reductionistic and assumes something as complex as the holistic education of a human can be reduced to job training. Educators fear that credentialing is now so dominant; corners are being cut in concerning ways. Fast-paced course compilation that is slavish to efficiency is achieving one goal at the expense of the other. Consequently, institutions are drifting too far from our moral and intellectual moorings. The fraying of society is the manifestation of trading a broad-based education focused on effective citizenship for a narrowly defined program of job training.

My other conversation partners are students, along with their parents, and employers. To be sure, parents are eager for their children to find professional accomplishment and economic success, but they also are committed to seeing them live a life of personal fulfillment. At the same time, employers are interested in the technical and professional potential in our graduates, but it is equally important to them that their employees be committed to

- learning as a lifestyle,
- contributing to the success of others,
- embracing creativity in the face of complexity, and
- understanding difference across diversity.

Parents and employers are persuasively articulate about the integration and alignment of education and workforce as they envision the service of an individual within a professional community of practice, as well as citizenship in the communities of family, neighborhood, faith, and civil society. Our best students understand this instinctually. They are committed to integrating their general, professional, and experiential learning by building on the foundation of their coursework with the essential elements of a broad-based educational design (Putnam 2022a).

Achieving the kind of precise results many policymakers are seeking is not possible. They continue to expect students will follow the incentives they create, pursue careers where there are workforce demands, and never change their minds. If they would only talk with students, they would learn a lot.

Learners Get to Choose

The contrast between the narrative of the Truman Report and the story told today is stark. An education for purposes of advancing democracy has a dual function to support engaged citizenship and prepare competent professionals. Both are necessary for the well-being of democracy. The reduction of students to workforce participants, however, is an attempt at fostering efficiency in the system for training workers. This is done at the expense of nurturing a meaningful role for individuals to serve in civil society, in addition to the contributions they make as workers. The imbalance is what the Truman Report argued against at a time when democracy was threatened by totalitarian domination. Accordingly, there is a vested interest in a democracy to see the development of citizens and workers as two sides of the same coin.

The reductionism of today goes even further, however. Not only does citizenship fade from our societal thinking as an organized priority, but our ideas about the workforce are being further reduced to only value workers in high-demand career fields. While the labor market strongly influences educational practice and policy, it is now pursued to the exclusion of equally important considerations for a democratic society.

As noted earlier, I was involved for several years as a member of the executive committee for a state-wide initiative called Future Ready Iowa. The effort served as a platform for articulating the integration of education, training, and workforce development for the state. The resulting programs have had many benefits, but also a few challenges. The early foundation for these activities was laid in Governor Terry Branstad's administration, during which time Governor Kim Reynolds (then lieutenant governor), served as the champion for the program. The Branstad and Reynolds administrations have made education and workforce a priority interest for the State of Iowa, despite constituent disagreements in policy and practice intended to achieve the desired aims.

Initiatives at this scale have many moving parts and involve many people. Most interesting to me, however, were deliberations in the various committees and task forces seeking to formulate programs and policies to advance workforce preparation and success. The various working groups were populated by policymakers, state agency leaders, business leaders, and educators. I found it fascinating to listen to the discussions. The driving force in almost all of the conversations was a need for workers in high-demand fields. From the perspective of employers and economic development leaders, this was the primary consideration. The dependency on the educators was to produce the educated and trained workforce, appropriately credentialed to fill these jobs, expand the economy, increase the tax base, and yield growing prosperity.

Many discussions focused on the various degrees, diplomas, certificates, credentials, licenses, registrations, micro-credentials, and badges needed to expand the desired workforce. There was an acknowledged need for funding through various student aid programs, including a last-dollar scholarship program for enrollment at Iowa's community colleges. Support for apprenticeships was also an important program development. It was an all-hands-on-deck approach with an if-we-build-it-they-will-come perspective. A few participants, however, consistently introduced a question about the pool of potential students from which we would draw this future, educated, and trained workforce: "What if they don't want to do it?" The typical response was, "These are good, high-paying jobs!" The obvious next question followed: "What if they don't want to go to school?"

Many potential candidates already made a decision to not pursue a postsecondary education path, perhaps some with regret. In such cases this could be a great opportunity. As the work of planning the initiative was completed, however, the realization emerged that in order for students who have avoided or delayed enrolling in a postsecondary program of study to find success, some barriers would need to be overcome. It was not just about financial aid. Some lacked adequate academic preparation. Some had family complexities difficult or impossible to manage. Cascading questions emerged: What about remediation? What about childcare? What about transportation? What about access to technology? How can we provide mentoring?

Despite these challenges, there were many virtues associated with the programs that have emerged through the years. They are, in fact, worthy pursuits in service of education and workforce needs in Iowa. The problem is that, in the end, people get to choose, and sometimes our best efforts fail to close the gap needed to bridge people to an educational experience that will prepare them for work in middle-skill settings, never mind more advanced technical and professional careers.

If I have one disappointment in my experience with Future Ready Iowa, it's that we were never able to elevate the discourse enough to understand a narrowly defined educational program does not endeavor to educate the whole person as contemplated by the Truman Report. The result will typically fall short of the ambitions of policymakers and business leaders.

Seen through the arc of time, the entire system of education is at issue. This is an old lament. For decades, policymakers have expressed concern about the "system" of education with little success in reshaping it. There is a reason for this. Our educational system has been built through time over centuries with some admittedly immovable foundational elements, but also with more pliable components that could be the focus of some efforts, if we put energy where it can be constructively applied (cathedrals). The challenge is change in a highly complex system happens gradually by assimilation (the Borg). The structures are diffused. No one is in charge. Gradual change is processed through loosely coupled connections that metabolize innovations by infusing them with traditions. Emerging ideas are adopted in a slow-paced process of conformity, which eventually becomes a pattern for standardization and convention. Failed attempts at sponsoring change on a systemic level are unsuccessful because inadequate consideration is given to the gnarly terrain to overcome in order to achieve a more comprehensive result (canal building). Patience is required to layer-in incremental levels of change. This kind of dedication is often not available. Fluid participation prevents the kind of continuity needed to pursue generations of change management through time.

Everything Belongs to Learning

The learner is an individual with unlimited complexity. The unfolding educational experience is necessarily structured to accommodate a generalized pattern of human development, but that does not erase the profoundly unique characteristics of each student. Likewise, the teacher, who is also a learner, brings all the complexities of their own educational and life journey. The well-intended systems of education provide a foundation and a framework into which we introduce millions of participants with an unfathomable level of interaction. The simple fact that there is a reasonable level of coherence in this process seems like a monumental achievement of its own. Expectations for uniformity, given this complicated reality, are too high, as is our desire for precision. It will never occur. No two educational journeys, like life experiences, are the same. It is enough that the body of knowledge has definitional contours allowing for the exchange of ideas.

There is strength in the accepted methods for teaching and learning appropriately adapted to various educational settings and contextually relevant to the learner or learners at hand. Despite their immense imperfections, standards are available to assess learning and progress toward an intended goal. Spaces and technologies exist to support learning appropriate to the learning needs presented. No learning system will ever map the level of complexity resident in learners. The task is to curate an appropriate learning experience despite the limitations. Policymakers and educators must admit that they cannot control that which is inherently uncontrollable. The alternative to control, however, is cooperation.

Cooperating with learning first requires an embrace of human development. Everything belongs to learning. Learning is not confined to formal settings like classrooms, labs, studios, and online platforms. These are suitable places to organize certain aspects of learning, but learning is not controlled there. Learning happens in a coffee shop. It happens on an athletic field. It happens in a community center. The list is endless. Students integrate the fullness of their life experience with the portions that are more formally designed. Cooperating with human development is an acknowledgment that students begin the journey as a fully dependent learner. Families are the first teachers, and the list of teachers gradually expands to include classroom teachers, coaches, and many others along the way. Teachers accumulate. The task of education is to help facilitate the journey of learning as a student gradually transitions through the arc of time to be an increasingly independent learner. The best teachers understand this and organize their teaching around it. It happens at different paces and with different approaches. While there are many tools, techniques, and technologies to support learning, the teaching and learning process is relational and remains a fundamentally human enterprise.

Second, cooperating with learning also requires an embrace of ambiguity. There is a long-standing program for eighth graders in Iowa called *I Have a Plan*. While there are benefits for very young students to begin exploring ideas about their future, my abiding concern about this program is that it attempts to focus student interest far too early in the developmental process. I speak here as a parent with an experience from 2011. Our then eighth-grade daughter, Greta, was sitting at the kitchen counter doing some schoolwork. I was sitting nearby reading. I had no idea what she was working on, but she turned to me and asked, "How do you spell Stanford?" Not even looking up from my book I replied, "S-T-A-N-F-O-R-D." A few minutes later she asked, "How do you spell Harvard?" I replied, "Greta, if you can't spell Harvard, you can't go there." She was working on her submission for the I Have a Plan program. Though I was not concerned such conversations were being initiated in school, I was concerned about the level of specificity she was asked to provide. The process ended with my wife, Tammy, and I joining Greta in a meeting at school with her homeroom teacher to discuss her plan. While the meeting was required, the teacher, also not a fan of the program, spent time with us talking about Greta's experience in school. Greta's vision for her life, as expressed in the eighth grade, and even through her years of high school, bears no resemblance to the very fulfilling life she has today. The intervening years were a time of self-discovery, which changed her perspective dramatically.

Cooperating with learning finally requires an embrace of flexibility. There are those who argue today's students are less prepared than previous generations. I think it is more accurate to say they are differently prepared. My faculty colleagues note they are frequently redesigning classes to accommodate these differences. There is a sense among some of a widening gap between where the students are at the point of entry and where they need to be, in preparation of launching professional careers or pursuing graduate and professional school opportunities. In some cases, this reflects the effects of standards-based grading in narrowing the teaching, learning, and assessment process to specified performance standards with repeated opportunities to resubmit assignments. For college faculty this feels like boundaries on the scope of learning for strong students, less focus on deep reading, less emphasis on analytic thinking, and less time for rigorous writing. Concurrent enrollment or dual credit can also play a role. Though there are benefits from advancing students with ability to pursue more challenging college-level coursework, the expanding course offerings are including students who are too young and not college-ready. Concerns persist about preparation for sequenced courses taken in college, as well as the sufficiency of retained learning required to advance to high levels of study.

Differences in student preparation always factor into student learning in college, but to many teachers these seem to be more pronounced. Such a range of backgrounds, however, requires more flexibility. Inclusive course design is an emerging conversation among faculty who are students of their own teaching practice. Accommodating many different students with individual needs and characteristics is daunting, but it is effective in supporting students as unique learners.

Embracing flexibility is also the task of the learner. Despite societal pressures, the riskiest path a student can follow today is to major in a job title. There is simply too much changing in the workplace as computerization, automation, and artificial intelligence continue to evolve. The extent of the changes coming to the workforce remain uncertain, but the advice I offer students is to major in adaptation. Whatever academic disciplines and professional fields of study they pursue, they are bound to encounter life and career disruptions. The combination of changes in workplace with the dynamics of everyday life make career targeting rather risky. I encourage students to slow down and not be in too much of a hurry. It's important they focus on the question of being (who they are becoming) as well as the question of doing (how they will animate their sense of being). This calls them to prepare for their future by amassing all the knowledge, skills, and experiences they can, and avoid the mistake of over-planning a future that will be shaped more by the unfolding of circumstance than it will be by their rigid intents. They should have many possible futures before them as a hedge against the risk that life may not be obedient to their wishes.

The answer to the question, "Who is the learner and what should they learn?" has as many answers as there are students. To be sure, there is expected content knowledge in professions that in some cases is very detailed, specific, and technical. In others a more generalized understanding of patterns and practices is suitable. Beyond the professional setting, and true for all students, is the need to be effective citizens in the families, communities, and workplaces served through the learning gains made. Attempts to understand learners, and design a meaning-ful learning experience for them, are still subject to their will-ingness to participate. Educators may think we control access to learning, the means by which learning occurs, and the assess-ment of whether learning has happened or not. But the learner is still in control of their use of time, energy, and money. They get to choose.

Learning is, by its very nature, expansive, and the learner is called to be an explorer. The body of knowledge in which the learner is released is vast, and the learner needs the guidance of other, more experienced learners—we call teachers—to navigate well. Learning requires a commitment of enormous amounts of time. Society grows impatient with this reality and wishes to change the question of "Who is the learner and what should they learn?" to "Where are the workers and how quickly can we make them productive?" The Truman Report posited an expansive view of education big enough to embrace both. The perspec-tive we see today yields a one-sided, imbalanced approach as the structures of the national higher education enterprise bind educators to rigid patterns of conformity and convention. There are times I am persuaded a societal agenda to make learning faster, cheaper, and job-focused is self-defeating. Learning has become more transactional and less relational. For many it is more about checking boxes than pursuing ambitions. The drive for entertainment crowds out the desire for inspiration. It is no wonder employers continue to express concern about the lack of soft skills—a committed work ethic, a practiced skill of working in teams, the determination to see a project through, willingness to take risks by expressing creativity and innovation, the cour-age to think critically and challenge the status quo. These are skills developed through the disciplines of learning forged through time.

Despite the justifiable expressions of concern related to learning in general, there are still impressive students on our campuses. I see them every day. More could be available if leaders were willing to undertake the hard work of change management through the arc of time. It is a generational task; one that requires repeated cycles of innovation, assimilation, conformity, and convention to unfold; a process that demands comprehensive planning and long-term, phased implementation beyond the career-span of any one leader. The structures of the postsecondary universe are intensely rigid. There are so many rules. It sometimes feels like we are the victims of other people's choices.

CHAPTER 9

My Hands Are Tied

During the late winter of 2022, I received a call from the president of the Iowa Association of Independent Colleges and Universities (IAICU), Gary Steinke. The Iowa legislature was in session, which begins in January each year and typically extends to June. This period is the "rainy season" for Gary, who represents the independent colleges of Iowa for both federal and state government relations. For several years I have served as the chair of the board of directors for IAICU, and calls from Gary are frequent during these months as legislation is introduced that intersects with the interests of the association.

This particular call was a heads-up that legislation regarding transgender athletes had been introduced in the Iowa House of Representatives (Iowa House File 2416). Initially, it appeared this was an interscholastic issue for local school systems in the state, but over the course of a few days it was extended to intercollegiate athletics beginning with our public universities in Iowa, then soon the independent colleges were added. Simply put, the legislation prohibited any educational institution in

Iowa from permitting the participation of a transgender female athlete on teams designated for "females, women, or girls." The operative language of the Iowa Code as adopted is as follows:

1. a. An interscholastic athletic team, sport or athletic event that is sponsored or sanctioned by an educational institution or organization must be designated as one of the following, based on the sex at birth of the participating students:

    (1) Females, women, or girls.

    (2) Males, men, or boys.

    (3) Coeducational or mixed.

   b. Only female students, based on their sex, may participate in any team, sport, or athletic event designated as being for females, women, or girls. (Iowa Code 2023)

News headlines at that time were drawing attention to the story of Lia Thomas, the NCAA Division I swimmer from the University of Pennsylvania. Thomas, a transgender female athlete, was competing on a women's swim team having previously competed on a men's swim team. This introduced a novel set of questions about the role gender identity and expression should play in sports. The debate was animated by the interaction of two different expressed concerns. The first was an issue of fairness that hinged on whether it was fair for a transgender female athlete to compete against female athletes in view of potential physiological differences; or whether it was fair to deny a transgender female athlete access to competition over a matter of gender identity, a potential act of sexual discrimination. These conflicting issues of fairness also interacted with deep religious and ideological differences of opinion regarding the status of the LGBTQ+ members of the American society. Colleges and universities were caught once again in the middle of conflicting mandates.

The legislation moved quickly through the process and was signed into law by the governor March 3, 2022. A few weeks after the bill was adopted, the IAICU board of directors, composed of the presidents of the member colleges in the association, met with elected state officials. This is customary during the season of the year when the legislature is in session. Our conversation with Governor Kim Reynolds turned to this topic among many others. Governor Reynolds outlined her support for the legislation as a matter of competitive fairness outweighing the attending concerns of potential sexual discrimination. The shared discussion around the matter was principled and thoughtful as various views were represented. In the end, the governor acknowledged this is a matter likely to be litigated through time as competing policy interests are explored. Also acknowledged was the complexity associated with a national patchwork of laws, the impact such laws would have on NCAA and NAIA interests across states, issues of interstate commerce, and practical matters of enforceability. The question I had for Governor Reynolds was, "What happens if a transgender female athlete travels to an Iowa college or university from an institution in another state that permits transgender female athletes to participate in women's sports?" Her interpretation was the Iowa law would not apply since it prohibits a transgender female athlete from participating on a team (i.e., included on a team roster) in any school or college located in Iowa. Accordingly, it would be possible for a transgender female athlete from Minnesota enrolled in an institution in that state to compete in Iowa. It would be equally possible for a transgender female athlete from Iowa who is enrolled at an institution in Minnesota to compete in Iowa. A key distinction in the intent and interpretation of the law is the difference between the organization of high school interscholastic competition being contained within the state, and the intercollegiate athletics universe extending well beyond state borders to regional and national competition. The original intent was targeted at high schools. The political reality, however, directed Iowa's colleges and universities to board the same bus, despite the fundamental differences in the competitive context.

In the weeks that followed, the NCAA began to inquire about the provisions in place to honor the rights of all students, including transgender athletes. The questionnaires included an interest in access to locker room and restroom facilities, local ordinances that could affect the experience of transgender student-athletes, and various institutional policies that could be at issue. The interest of the NCAA was fundamentally about postseason play drawing teams from multiple states, and the extent to which an institution in a state with restrictions on the participation of transgender student-athletes might cascade down to teams participating in an NCAA postseason event hosted on a particular campus. Looming was a potential decision to prohibit an institution from hosting an NCAA event if certain conditions were not adequately met.

Pending still are questions about how the US Department of Education will seek to interpret the Title IX regulations related to sexual discrimination and the litigation that may emerge over years. The manner in which the NCAA and/or NAIA may address these interests and concerns, along with the sport-specific associations that play a role in setting the rules and regulations related to competition, remains a work in progress. This trickles down to individual athletic conferences as well since some conferences include institutions from different states. The matter is far from resolution and will be processed through the long arc of time.

In the meantime, the resulting ambiguities persist. Colleges and universities are caught in the middle of competing interests and demands for compliance. The risk of being targeted in litigation is pronounced and the degrees of freedom quite limited. If the US Department of Education issues a revision of Title IX policies prohibiting discrimination of transgender students, such a decision would presumably have the force of law at the federal level and void state laws to the contrary. Institutions in this example would be trapped in an unresolved legal dispute that could extend for years. Making the matter more complicated, an election that leads to a change in administration or the control of the legislature at the federal or state level could change the legal and regulatory framework as the political winds blow. This happened in the transition from the Obama administration to the Trump administration when Title IX regulations were substantively changed. Current and future administrative actions on Title IX policies could lead to recurring revisions.

The specific examples offered above are not the point, however. The dynamics of the system surrounding postsecondary institutions is the real issue. This condition, multiplied across all the external entities seeking to impact policies and practices at the institutional level, binds colleges and universities in an undefined and uncontrolled system of interactions that must be continually reconciled. The experience for college and university presidents is a life playing Whac-A-Mole.

The cascading effects of external dynamics also impact internal realities as campus constituencies express views about controversial matters and expect the institution with which they are affiliated to behave in a manner consistent with their individual perspective. In the fall of 2022, I was in a conversation with a group of alumni during our homecoming activities. A question surfaced about the new transgender female athlete law in Iowa, but it was misstated to suggest the state had implemented a ban on all transgender student-athlete participation in schools and colleges in Iowa. Those in the room had differing opinions on the law, but the bigger challenge was they did not understand the law. I corrected the premise of the question first by noting the law only applied to transgender female athletes on teams designated for "females, women, or girls," not to all transgendered athletes on all teams. My clarification was met with bewilderment. I noted the law also was limited to the participation of athletes enrolled in schools and colleges located in Iowa. Confusion greeted this clarification. To help bring additional clarity, I reported on our IAICU meeting with the governor, noting the interpretation we received was that if a transgendered female athlete comes to our campus to compete from an institution located in another state, then the law does not apply. Bewilderment and confusion turned into blank stares.

A similar confusion emerged at a later time, when Central College hosted Luther College (also located in Iowa) for a women's softball game. Included on the roster for Luther was a student-athlete who identified as male. Some attending the game contacted our athletics director to express concern this had been allowed, in violation of state law. Until he explained it to them, they did not realize the law had been narrowly tailored to thread a needle between the competing interests of competitive fairness and sexual discrimination, and it was accordingly limited in scope.

The Spaghetti Chart

The number of external entities staking a claim on the policies and processes of higher education is breathtaking. The list includes the categories such as federal, state, and local governments involving an untold number of agencies, offices, departments, and jurisdictions seeking to shape and define the work of educators through an array of legal, regulatory, policy, and financial frameworks. Regional organizations and compacts designed to coordinate cross-state activities add to this mix. Dozens of accreditors, both regional and professional, have standards to be applied at the institutional level, each of their own design and purpose. Institutional, academic, and professional associations in the postsecondary landscape abound and seek to establish and maintain best practices. Foundations look to influence the direction of higher education by way of their philanthropy. Athletics associations set rules and boundaries with consequences for institutional operations. Religious affiliations and other defining relationships set expectations for how an institution will conduct itself. Together, these external entities represent hundreds, perhaps thousands, of points of reconciliation for colleges and universities. It can only be described as a spaghetti chart.

The combined content presented by these entities is encyclopedic in scope and completely inaccessible for the uninitiated. It's a culture in which jargon is a native language and acronyms abound. Most importantly, it's a universe of activity where conformity and convention combine to provide the force of gravity that holds it all together. This is a self-referential enterprise contained within a closed intellectual universe. There is limited tolerance for anything that changes the status quo too quickly or too comprehensively. The system is not in anyone's control and moves in a stimulus-response pattern. An emergent idea is vetted unpredictably through a meandering path of interactions and communications. Some of these are formal; many are informal. Occasionally something seemingly new surfaces, but it is rarely new. It tends to be refreshed jargon repackaged for a new generation with a sprinkle of new technology added, and almost always with a new acronym. An innovation is declared to be both new and profound. The problem, as the adage reminds us, is that "what is new is not profound and what is profound is not new."

Critics of this perspective suggest it is just cynicism. To the contrary, I find hope in the realization that there are immense virtues in the national enterprise of higher education. Despite its many vices, it is notably durable. It is designed to be built over generations, allow for gradual development, and last a very long time. It never quite feels like it's done, much like a cathedral. Change comes by assimilation as illustrated by the Borg. New ideas are processed through an undefinable and complex network that adapts to change slowly, but reliably. It requires intense planning and staged effort to create the conditions in which a big idea can be implemented. Planning in higher education seems to be a task consistent with the scale of building a canal in an unforgiving landscape.

Letting go of the eye-rolling lament regarding these conditions is the first step forward. The "system" of the postsecondary universe is not going to suddenly be revised despite our protests regarding its recalcitrance and inefficiency. If anything, it will become more complex through time, reflecting the increasing complexity of society. It's enough to seek incremental change. Even with a gradual approach, however, it's easy to get lost in a system of this scale given its complexity. The tendency of actors in this enterprise is to focus on the moving parts and tinker with the mechanisms by which they are manipulated. This practice results in a lot of activity but produces little in the way of meaningful improvement. A better focus would be on studying antecedents to the present conditions, the foundational elements that make them unyielding, and the fundamental characteristics of design. From there it is possible to change the condition through time by assimilation. The patient discipline required to treat the underlying condition rather than the symptoms begins with the acknowledgment that pursuing the initiative intended will take time. Otherwise, the tyranny of the urgent intensifies the exasperation of innovators seeking change. The details of process then dominate the discourse and the reason for undertaking the effort in the first place is lost—another version of the means-end reversal. A return to the essential questions of higher education is a place to begin.

The Essential Question of Participation

Who is permitted or enabled to participate in the experience of higher education? For some this is a long-settled matter and hardly worth deliberation. In their view, everyone should have the opportunity to pursue a postsecondary educational experience. As a national consensus, however, this assertion is undermined by a counternarrative, which if stated plainly would say, "It depends. Does everyone really need a higher education?"

According to the 2023 figures reported in the *Digest of Education Statistics* (NCES n.d.c, Table 104.10), in 1910, 2.7% of the US population above the age of 25 had earned a baccalaureate degree. By 2023, that number reached 38.3%. Undoubtedly, over the past century the United States has witnessed a significant expansion in baccalaureate degree attainment. Entry into higher education as a high school graduate also has increased through time, though the rate of entry today is on the decline. In 1960,

45.1% of high school completers enrolled in college. From 2004 to 2019, that percentage ranged between 65% and 70%. From 2020 to 2022, the rate of college enrollment declined to approximately 62%. It is likely some COVID-19 pandemic effects are present in these percentages, but it is not clear these figures will return to previous levels (NCES n.d.d, Table 320.20). Other factors impacting participation rates—including concerns regarding potential student loan debt, direct job opportunities out of high school, or cultural assumptions regarding the efficacy of postsecondary education—are all subjects of speculation in assessing enrollment patterns. Nothing definitive can be claimed regarding future trends. Levels of attrition among college students is also a consistent area of concern. The disparity between those entering college and those attaining a degree, as noted in the percentages above, suggests an approximate completion rate for entering cohorts just above 50%.

I have noted throughout this writing the importance of the Truman Commission Report, as it laid out a conceptual blueprint for the development and expansion of the postsecondary education universe in the wake of World War II. The report's foundational expectation anticipated an increase in the national need and individual demand for advanced training and education for the American citizenry. The President's Commission on Higher Education, which produced the report, included in its analysis the results of the National Inventory of Talent. The report states:

> Upon these considerations this Commission bases what it believes to be conservative estimates of the proportions of the population with reasonable expectations of completing higher education at specific levels. These proportions which constitute this Commission's "National Inventory of Talent" are:

1. At least 49 percent of our population has the mental ability to complete 14 years of schooling with a curriculum of general and vocational studies that should lead either to gainful employment or to further study at a more advanced level.
2. At least 32 percent of our population has the mental ability to complete an advanced liberal or specialized professional education.

If these proportions of American youth are to be admitted to institutions of higher education, we shall have to provide a much greater variety of institutions and programs than we now have to meet their needs. But the Commission has no way of estimating what effect such modifications of the existing system might have on the number of students to be expected.

The probable shift in social attitudes toward the desirability of increased education, together with economic aid, will lead more people to complete additional years of schooling. These factors would undoubtedly increase the proportions in the "inventory," making the estimates not only conservative but probably minimal. (President's Commission 1947, vol. 1, 41–42)

The report's framing of the analysis for future enrollment patterns in the decades that followed proved to be remarkably accurate. Population growth through the baby boom era was already recognized as a factor in demand, but the recognition of the growing professional and social expectations for higher learning were astutely insightful. The report continues:

To provide adequately for this near doubling of the student load in higher education will require a proportionate expansion and improvement of our educational plant, equipment and personnel.

We may be sure that the private colleges and universities will, in the future as in the past, contribute immeasurably to the expansion and improvement of our facilities for higher education, and it is to be hoped that they will be able to find the necessary funds without increasing the cost to the individual. But in the nature of things, the major burden for equalizing educational opportunity must rest on publicly supported institutions. (President's Commission 1947, vol. 1, 44)

As noted in chapter 2, the Truman Report was never enacted as a matter of comprehensive federal legislation and was criticized for its overreach, but it presented an influential framework through the arc of time. The report wrestled with the extent to which the population would seek to pursue more advanced education, but it presaged an unfolding reality American society witnessed through the decades since.

The debate about who should be permitted or enabled to enroll in college is reemerging, but with a different set of assumptions. The essential question of access and opportunity is at the core. This question, however, is not new. The Truman Report predates the US Supreme Court's 1954 *Brown v. Board of Education* decision ending de jure racial segregation in schools, the 1961 executive order issued by President John F. Kennedy initiating affirmative action policies in the federal administration, and the Civil Rights Act of 1964. The report, however, anticipates a widening diversity in higher education years earlier and condemned racial discrimination in very clear terms. The report states:

Discrimination in the admission of college students because of an individual's race, creed, color, sex, national origin, or ancestry is an antidemocratic practice which creates serious inequalities in the opportunity for higher education. The Commission is opposed to discrimination and believes it should be abandoned. (President's Commission 1947, vol. 1, 25)

In addition to anticipating the eventual rejection of discriminatory practices too commonly employed at that time, the commission noted the educational dimensions of inclusivity in the higher education context:

As we bring more and more students to the campus, we shall increase in proportion the tremendous variety of human and social needs the college programs must meet. We shall add to the already overwhelming diversity of aptitudes, interests, and levels of attainment that characterize the college student body. And so we shall have to increase the diversification of curricular offerings and teaching methods to correspond.

Yet in the midst of all the necessary diversity we must somehow preserve and expand a central unity. We must make sure that the education of every student includes the kind of learning and experience that is essential to for free men [and women] to live in a free society. (President's Commission 1947, vol. 1, 45–46)

As the years passed, the practices of affirmative action in college admission are now in transition due to the 2023 Supreme Court ruling from *Students for Fair Admissions (SFFA) v. Harvard* and *SFFA v. University of North Carolina*. Questions regarding the societal interest in creating the opportunity for participation in higher education are now a bit more complicated. The issues raised in 1947 regarding the anticipated need in society for higher education must now be reassessed and reformulated as we anticipate 2027, 2037, and beyond. Whatever interventions or incentives policymakers and institutional leaders employ, these considerations will become the foundation to long-term planning and decision-making in the coming years and will have a binding effect on colleges and universities. Consider the following:

Is it desirable that as many students as possible enroll in some form of postsecondary education to promote the virtues of a free society?

Do workforce demands necessitate the advanced education of citizens for roles in organizations, institutions, and businesses?

Should the conferring of social status be a motivation for pursuing an advanced education in American society?

To what extent is knowledge for its own sake manifested through personal inquiry and fulfillment an interest of society in enabling participation in higher education?

Have the patterns of the past 75 years taught us there is an upper limit to the interest and demand for postsecondary education among American citizens?

Is it possible that America already has seen the peak of participation and completion rates among students in our colleges and universities?

Any national consensus that may have existed for a time has devolved into a swirling ambiguity of purpose. In the absence of a broadly accepted agenda among policymakers and institutional leaders, market forces will determine the future patterns of enrollment and the consequences, intended or not, for the size and shape of the national higher education enterprise. Who is permitted or enabled to enroll will continue to be a function of individual agency and mobility in the marketplace, leading to intensifying competition among institutions. The limitations of resources in an enterprise that relies heavily on the subsidies of appropriations, gifts, grants, and contracts to function, in addition to student-related revenue, will provide few degrees of freedom at the institutional level. As population growth stagnates, participation rates may remain stubbornly limited. The confluence of interests and expectations among the many stakeholders in asserting who should be permitted or enabled to enroll is further confounded by a marketplace that manifests the aggregation of individual choices made by millions of students. The combined force of external pressures is stifling for institutions seeking to be all things to all people in a setting in which there is no shared agenda to pursue.

The Essential Question of Affordability

For decades, tuition pricing has been a source of great consternation across the postsecondary universe of policymakers, policy analysts, accreditors, associations, and institutional leaders.

There is no agreement among the various players on the causes and effects of the escalating prices. Some analysts blame the availability of state and federal aid in the form of grants and loans to students as the enabler of institutions harvesting public funding, and still increasing prices for families. Institutions claim inflationary pressures and market expectations for programs and services have exacerbated the "cost disease" economists commonly identify with labor-intensive professional firms plagued with high labor costs and few economies of scale. In response, colleges and universities utilize funded and unfunded discounts (student aid) to offset the escalating sticker prices in a buyer's market impacted by declining demographics and decreasing participation. This produces a growing dependency on endowment spending, annual giving, and budget reallocations to fund discounts. Such a pricing structure rests on increases in enrollment to produce net revenue margins. The result is operating budget deficits. Financial institutions including banks, auditors, bond raters, federal and state agencies, and professional associations decry the discount rates and budget deficits. Concurrently, consumers cheer enormous financial aid packages, seek to avoid loans, want past loans forgiven, and lobby for free college access. Public universities point to the erosion of state appropriations in contrast with dramatic increases in operating costs as the driver of tuition increases. Legislators complain about runaway spending. On and on it goes.

The solution asserted by policymakers is accountability. More consumer information in the form of net tuition price calculators, standardized financial aid award letters, and disclosures regarding average student debt are imposed. More research studies are pursued on tuition pricing and student outcomes. Policies related to the assurance of transfer credit, student aid focused on high-demand careers, and dual credit enrollment are all examples of peripheral interventions to affect pricing. Many task forces, committees, commissions, and blue-ribbon panels have been convened across the higher education landscape to discuss the problem of increasing tuition prices. The products are detailed reports and research briefs with findings and recommendations. Little of this material is read beyond a scan of the executive summary. Yet considerable time, energy, and money is devoted to these projects. The intent is admirable; the overall benefit negligible.

Real-time tuition pricing decisions are undertaken at the institutional or system level. Such decisions are informed by patterns in various market segments, comparative and trend analyses among competitors with high levels of overlap in applied and admitted students, and idiosyncratic institutional needs based on wealth, indebtedness, regional cost structures, and infrastructure demands. The process is a cobbling together of independent factors influenced by a subjective analysis purposed to maintain some reasonable level of equilibrium. A tuition pricing decision is a tactical choice made months or even a year in advance of its implementation, and it remains in force for a year until the next round. Thus, each pricing process occupies a two-year window, and little can be done to change it once announced.

Policymakers and analysts insist the business model for higher education is broken and needs to change. No one is in charge. No one has the authority to issue a decree. Since the 19th century, higher education has been a marketplace. The evolution of the national higher education enterprise has only intensified these forces. Today, a convergence of these market forces is a natural consequence of the dynamics of growth and change through time. Short of a forced federal takeover of the entire postsecondary universe, there is no path by which the naturally unfolding effects of diffused decision-making, distributed authority, and disparate agenda setting can be overcome. The marketplace of colleges and universities informed by the many interests of individual institutions and the interventions of many external entities will determine the size and shape of the market, the winners and losers in the market, and the programmatic scope of the market. No amount of complaining will change this dynamic. The opportunity to manage this through the long arc of time begins with the realization this situation cannot be addressed by attempting to assert control. Change comes with patient exercise of influence and the sponsorship of assimilation. Until and unless a wider narrative for higher education is reestablished, with a concurrent understanding that change will take time and will not avoid immediate consequences, the system will continue to press institutions into conformity and convention.

Is There a Way to Break Free?

The postsecondary universe by its nature fragments everything it encounters. That is how the task orders set before the enterprise are accomplished. The benefit of this approach is that breaking the work down into bite-size chunks supports assimilation. Getting lost in this maelstrom, however, is the unfortunate risk. Elevating the discourse surrounding assimilation is the means by which a sustained effort can be maintained by generations of participants. The stonecutters who worked on the Cathedral of St. John the Divine, as described in chapter 1, knew they were working on something much bigger than the immediate task at hand. That did not distract them from the artisanship of the moment. It did provide a larger narrative in which the work was meaningful and purposeful, encouraging long-term thinking and planning.

The narrative for higher learning in America has been lost to time. The key elements of that narrative remain, but a commonly held overarching purpose is no longer discernable within the frenetic activity dominating the enterprise. Recovering historical themes can serve in elevating the discourse and recovering the national narrative for postsecondary education. It will take immense determination to make this possible, and only time will tell if it can succeed.

CHAPTER 10

Time Will Tell

During the 1992–93 academic year, I was deep into work on my dissertation, focused on struggling colleges facing the potential of closure or merger and the information trustees used to support decision-making under extreme conditions. After completing an extended onsite interview with the president of an institution struggling for survival, this seasoned college leader turned to me and asked, "Aren't you afraid you will become known as the college coroner?" It was a chilling question. Though I avoided such a morbid professional pathway, I never lost my interest in the dynamics of institutional decline and the risk of demise.

I was grateful on my dissertation journey to have several thought partners along the way. One was Katharine Hanson, who served as the president of the Consortium on Financing Higher Education (COFHE, pronounced *co-fee*) from 1976–2002. She was generous with her time through a long phone conversation about my research. COFHE was formed in the mid-1970s with members from the most highly selective colleges and universities in America. The organization is a consortium providing data collection, analysis, and research on various aspects of finance, enrollment, and assessment for its members.

During the conversation, I asked Kay a simple question: "Why do colleges close?" Her response was, "Three reasons: money, mismanagement, and mattering." As she delved into the topic, she noted the dimension of money took various forms, most commonly a decline in enrollment. At the time we were speaking, the higher education enterprise had been experiencing the effects of the baby bust following the baby boom. The dimension of mismanagement also expressed itself in unique ways, but it was often associated with overextending the reach of ambition beyond an institution's capacity. At that time, the ignorance or denial of demographic realities was a common problem leading to unfortunate management decisions assuming more market strength than the reality supported. The most interesting dimension she described was this intriguing concept of mattering. Kay described it as the conditions presented when a college or university no longer matters to the constituency that founded it. Several obvious examples came to mind immediately. While colleges dedicated to serving gender-specific populations (i.e., colleges for men or women) still exist today, many moved to coeducational enrollment, some lacking sufficient enrollment (money) sought merger or acquisition opportunities, and others closed. These institutions no longer mattered sufficiently to the constituency that founded them, or for whom they were dedicated. Likewise, various religiously affiliated institutions were notably under stress during those years and faced challenges as church or denominational affiliations, rooted in the very distant past, were no longer as relevant in the contemporary society.

Now 30 years later, I am seeing the same dynamics at work in the current postsecondary universe. Money is tight across most sectors of higher education as participation from a shrinking demographic pool recedes. Misguided management decisions increasingly are consequential given the broad-based financial stress in the industry. Once again, unrealistic enrollment and fundraising goals are a concern. Mattering remains a potent reality for both public and private institutions. State appropriations have not kept pace with the expanding operational cost of public colleges and universities, to the point many in leadership of that sector ask, "Do we still matter to this state?" Private institutions with a dependency on a church affiliation, local community, or specialized profession ask the same question, "Do we still matter?"

One of my other conversation partners in the early 1990s was Joe O'Neill. Joe wrote a book in 1980 with his coauthor, Samuel Barnett, titled *Colleges and Corporate Change: Merger, Bankruptcy, and Closing, A Sourcebook for Trustees and Administrators*. During a phone call, I asked Joe the same question I put to Kay: "Why do colleges close?" His short answer was, "They run out of cash." The conversation, along with a careful reading of the book, offered deeper insights. My dissertation research included their work in examining the characteristics of an institution on the brink:

> First, is the issue of short-term term debt. Since small colleges often rely heavily on tuition for income, the pattern of their revenues is concentrated at the beginning of each term of attendance. As a result, there are times during the year when cash is exhausted and student accounts are in arrears, when an institution is forced to borrow from the bank to meet its financial obligations. The time can come, however, when a college fighting for its life in the midst of a declining enrollment will degenerate to the point

where banks will not be willing to renegotiate the institution's debt. Ultimately, the availability of funds reaches its limit, deficits become overwhelming, and options for survival disappear.

The second issue a declining institution faces is a tendency to over-estimate potential income. Trustees must be discriminating as administrators begin to project enrollment figures and development giving at levels that are unprecedented or unlikely given the circumstances. . . .

Third, there is a point at which the challenges that face an institution deteriorate its condition so severely that little can be done to prevent failure. . . . The situation is one in which every action taken to intervene on the institution's behalf actually weakens the position further. (Putnam 1994, 55–56)

In a later article, Joe noted:

Presidents feel free to concentrate on remedying the college's weaknesses and making institutional needs known to the board and to donors. Once, however, an institution begins to have money troubles, the open door to financial information closes swiftly. . . .

One of the paradoxes of college administration is that a president can talk to the board about the college's weak points only when the institution as a whole is sound. Once the institution begins to run deficits in its current account, presidential weakness becomes identified with institutional weakness. Then presidents concentrate on the hopeful signs of a turnaround. (O'Neill 1983, 27)

Joe's writing, now more than 40 years in the past, could be written today. It rhymes. The conditions are not exactly the same, but they are close enough to listen to these voices from decades ago and draw wisdom from them for the present. There are institutions today following the patterns identified decades ago. As the threshold of viability approaches a campus, the words Kay and Joe shared with me remain at the forefront of my thinking. For some colleges and universities on the brink, there is little that can be done once inertia takes over. Institutions in sufficient distress cannot cut, borrow, and discount their way to survival. For those with remaining degrees of freedom to act, the choices made may either accelerate decline or arrest downward pressure. Such decisions weigh heavily. In these circumstances there is benefit in taking a step back to see the broad patterns of the past, consider how they may be informing the present, and assess the extent to which the urgent interventions of the moment are a frenetic churn or a turn toward fundamental positive change.

Hitting the Pause Button

Considerable anxiety about the future of American higher education exists today as it did in the 1980s and 1990s, but policymakers and institutional leaders are at a disadvantage in deliberating these important matters. Few know much about or have an interpretive understanding of the history of American higher education and the attending organizational developments that have informed emerging conditions. Most dismiss such interests as dated and irrelevant, and yet express disappointment in the lack of progress. Unfortunately, there is insufficient awareness among leaders of how change is sponsored and processed in the national enterprise for higher education, resulting in faulty assumptions about the purported recalcitrance of postsecondary institutions and systems to respond. The same is true for institutions. The knee-jerk reaction is to overgeneralize the situation and seek simplistic explanations, such as blaming the faculty for holding institutions back. Given the number of false starts, aborted attempts, and misguided ideas for large-scale change littering the higher education landscape, it's prudent to stop and take a closer look. A well-informed but intellectually modest posture serves well in contemplating where this vast enterprise can and should move in the decades ahead, as it carries with it all the accumulated work of the past.

Repeated through the preceding chapters are three themes, represented by three images of organization, noted as patterns in the experience of colleges and universities through the arc of time. First, these institutions take a long time to build and then return the favor by lasting a long time. As such they are always a work in progress, generation after generation. The image of a cathedral serves as an example, with the qualities of time and endurance obvious characteristics. Second, change occurs through assimilation as novel ideas are processed through dif-fused interactions across the higher education enterprise, result-ing in a recursive pattern of gradual adoption followed by seasons of conformity and convention. My favorite space aliens, the Borg, are a model for assimilation. Third, large-scale interven-tions at the industry or institutional level require staging or phasing over long periods, with an early emphasis on creating the general conditions for success through time. The image of canal building, particularly the Panama Canal, is a reminder of how an ultimate goal is often dependent on many layers of change management implemented through time.

The call I extend to the higher education community is to ac-cept the reality of how change is facilitated in our context and cooperate with it. The best example of how this was initiated in a previous generation was the Truman Commission Report.

Despite its flaws and limitations, it collected the stirring interests emerging across the higher education landscape in the years following World War II. It was not definitive, though it set forth an agenda. It was not exhaustive, though it was comprehensive. It was not authoritative, in that it lacked any power to enact change, but it was compelling in offering arguments for how the higher education enterprise should evolve. We would benefit today from a similar effort, but it would need to take on a very different character. The late 1940s anticipated a period of impressive growth that continued for several decades. The failure of our national leaders in the interim is that a renewal of purpose was never crafted along the way as it became clear the earlier ambition had run its course. A renewed focus would not be about expansion. It would be about prioritization and reduction in scope. The potential benefit would be an agenda for change, despite the immensely painful experience of transition and contraction. Facilitating the change process and providing pathways for supporting discourse about the future could moderate the anxiety of many institutions and systems, and edge us toward solution-thinking as a national enterprise.

The default position for colleges and universities is the marketplace for higher education will decide the future. Some institutions will conclude their important work in the years ahead, some will reorganize or reposition to remain competitive, and some will find continued success through sufficient resource and market strength. More cries will come from institutions crossing the threshold of viability, pleading for state or federal funding to sustain them in their important missions and in service of the communities that depend on them.

It is highly unlikely a renewed national agenda would change the present course since the enterprise is deeply enmeshed in the dynamics of the marketplace. It would, however, serve as a means for imagining a potential future for which institutions can aim for the next decades. Difficult decisions loom large. Other industries have done this, some demonstrating better skill than others. There are lessons in considering how industries in transition behave. While individual entities within an industry may fail, survive, or thrive through time, the industries themselves endure. Higher education will be no different. The postsecondary universe will change through time, but it will not disappear. Such a change process will take a lot longer than most pundits think it will.

Higher Education as an Industry in Distress

Viewed as an industry, higher education is facing many of the same types of challenges encountered by other industries. External pressures converged to create widespread impacts as internal management struggled to respond to emerging conditions. Farming, auto manufacturing, air travel, health care, banking, insurance, real estate, retail, restaurants, entertainment, and many more have endured extended periods of change often in a recursive pattern. They have been impacted by the same Six-Pack of Change categories identified in chapter 4: demographic decline, economic uncertainty, workforce expectations, technological innovation, societal norms, and public policy. Each could articulate how these six factors have combined to form threats that exposed vulnerabilities. There is nothing new here. Each of these industries has survived, albeit with changes in the way the industry operates. Higher education is often compared to these industries as a form of criticism regarding its seeming inability to manage change. An honest appraisal of the arc of time applied to these industries, however, defies the perception that fundamental change was rapid. This is a misperception.

Banking, for all the technologies now applied to the industry, still has customers, accounts, regulations, and branches. The essential elements remain the same since the base concepts of the business remain intact. Airlines still have passengers, flight attendants, pilots, avionic technicians, ground crews, equipment, and airports. Health care has patients, doctors, prescription drugs, hospitals, medical equipment, medical procedures, and insurance. The auto industry still has plants and equipment, raw materials, assembly workers, engineers, transport, dealerships, and financing. Farming has farmers, markets, land, seeds, fertilizers, and equipment. Despite all the change present to these, and, in fact, all industries through the years, the industries remain active in society in essentially the same form, though with evolving technologies and organizational designs. Not all individual farms, hospital systems, airlines, entertainment companies, retail, and restaurant establishments have survived, however. Perhaps external conditions were too unfavorable or internal capacities not up to the presenting challenges. In the end, the markets re-sorted these industries, each in their own time.

The pace of change associated with these industries has had a long arc of time to be expressed. Banking endured the savings and loan crisis through the 1980s and 1990s. More than 1,000 of these institutions (about 32%) failed over a period of about 10 years. This yielded changes in the regulatory structures, but the essential elements of the banking industry remain. Patrons still visit local bank branches to obtain service, even as online portals offer concurrent convenience.

Patient care changed to take on a more team-based approach, with the efforts of doctors focused on specific tasks as physician assistants, nurse practitioners, and pharmacists play evolving roles. These are important adaptations, but highly trained practitioners still spend time with patients in examination rooms, and patients continue to visit pharmacies to collect prescription drugs.

Cable television first surfaced in the 1940s as a new technology, but it took more than 50 years before cable subscriptions reached their peak level, around 2000. The transition to streaming technologies, made possible by advancing internet technologies, now takes hold as cable subscription declines. What hasn't changed is a market for entertainment delivered to a home-based device. That aspect of the industry is stable, perhaps even timeless since the advent of radio.

Higher education still has students, teachers, instructional settings, resource materials, courses, grades, transcripts, and degrees. The structural elements for the enterprise as we know it today have foundations centuries old, but they began to adopt their present form in the 1940s. The postsecondary universe has expanded dramatically, reaching its enrollment peak in about 2010 as the echo baby boom moved through the school system. The industry of higher education evolves. Technologies gradually are adopted, and societal demands have evolved. Academic courseware, classroom technologies, remote access, and online programs are all ubiquitous on campuses today. In this way, higher education resembles other industries in which the core foundations remain but the organizational systems change.

Despite these similarities among industries, there is a specific condition more pertinent to higher education when compared to others that is worth exploring—population demographics. Higher education is highly dependent on birth rates. Despite the drive for lifelong learning, the concentration of activity remains on the years of late adolescence and young adulthood. The simple reality is birth rates in America fluctuated intensely from the baby boom to the baby bust to the echo boom. This has been followed by declining fertility rates projected to remain below replacement levels for decades to come. If this pattern had not emerged, we would be having a different national conversation. The single factor driving the necessity for change in higher education is that the scale of the system we have is too large for the existing population and the population we can reasonably project for the future. Most of the symptoms we want to treat as an industry are a derivative of this one underlying condition. The escalating cost of operation, excessive discount rates, hyper competition, and expanding capital expenses are driven by one thing: more students are required to sustain the scale of this national enterprise. The problem is they don't exist.

The Marketplace for Students

Students represent a specific type of participant consumer, pursuing a high-cost multiyear experience, with lasting effects on subsequent professional opportunities that in all likelihood will last a lifetime. An ongoing relationship with the institution is a common goal long after the consumer relationship is complete. A successful result yields alumni donors eager to see others pursue the opportunities they enjoyed. Individual identity is connected to brand strength as the reputation of the institution may rub off on the graduate. The acquisition of a student is costly and placing increased pressure on retaining each student through degree completion. Yet student retention is, in part, a function of their performance against academic and behavioral standards set by the institution. It's a complicated interaction—student and college give and receive in a reciprocal relationship. Both bring resources to the table. Students pay fees and institutions raise subsidy from external sources to underwrite a portion of the cost of education. The business model for higher education rests entirely on the presence and participation of students.

With fewer students entering the marketplace and the acquisition cost increasing rapidly, the competitive landscape yielded increasingly expensive programs, services, activities, and amenities. Student recruitment today involves an impressive array of marketing professionals, consultants, and associated operating budgets. The admissions office, once a drawer in the registrar's desk, is now a highly staffed, highly technical sales operation costing millions of dollars. This is not enough, however, as deep tuition discounts presently are required to attract students to most institutions, not because of an inability to pay a price consistent with the inherent expense base, but an unwillingness to pay what would be needed for institutions to maintain financial equilibrium. The financial picture in many institutions is upside down. Colleges and universities, both public and private, have always charged students less than it costs to educate them, given the benefits of appropriations, the generosity of donors, and accumulated endowment resources supporting current operating budgets. As many have noted, the current economic condition is unsustainable. Institutions in many parts of the country are edging toward the threshold of viability; they seek to avoid falling prey to the inertia drawing them toward the death spiral of collapsing quality.

The seeds of the current higher education marketplace were sown decades ago. No exit strategy was considered beyond the expansion era of higher education. Some may have assumed both federal and state governments would permanently sustain the system once fully established. Widening economic pressures across the levels of government, however, have allocated resources to other priorities, making little new funding available for higher education. It has presented itself as a perfect storm: intense competition for students reducing net revenue per student, increasing costs of operation in all categories of expense, and growing demands for capital expenditures for infrastructure and technology. To this point, the institutional response has been predictable. Cycles of audacity and austerity have taken hold. Bold announcements of periodic enrollment success are betrayed by financial statements revealing increasing fiscal stress.

Many have noted this unrelenting condition. Some argue the business model for higher education must be changed, but who will declare this new agenda for change and require its implementation? There is no central authority charged with the responsibility to do so. Others argue for voluntary mergers, acquisitions, and contractual affiliations. The conditions needed for these to work are difficult to find and even harder to manage. Institutions are loathe to give up their autonomy and even less inclined to give up their identity. When institutions are in close proximity, the odds of success increase but are by no means assured. Distant acquisitions of failing institutions exist but are rare. Shared administrative and academic agreements across institutions require change processes at each of the institutions seeking an affiliation. These are notoriously hard to negotiate and even harder to implement as existing commitments to faculty, staff, and vendors yield resistance with a determination to preserve the status quo. The simple reality is no institution will concede its independence, autonomy, or identity until and unless there is absolutely no other option. By that time, it is often too late to act. In many industries, merger and acquisition activity is seen as a positive step for preserving shareholder value, optimizing the use of assets, creating efficiency in operations, and moving an industry forward. There are structures and incentives for pursuing such a path. Banking, for example, is an industry that has the capacity for realigning markets for greater efficiency through mergers and acquisitions. Higher education has no inherent capacity and is unlikely to build such a skill set in the coming years.

Absent any intervention, the higher education marketplace will sort itself through the arc of time. Pundits sometimes make generalized statements about the future sorting process. There are arguments that residential campuses will cease to exist because they are just too expensive. While the expense realities are real, there is still a market for campus-based education, and that will endure. It may be a smaller market than 15 years ago, but it remains a strong and vibrant market among high school graduates pursuing the life experience associated with the traditional years of college. Other generalized predictions assert postsecondary education will move predominantly to online formats. This claim fails as many students at all levels of education express their personal dislike for courses taught online. High attrition rates suggest this may be cause for concern if reliable completion patterns cannot be established. The decreased size of the marketplace has not changed the preferences expressed by prospective students. They will continue to sort themselves into the various kinds of learning experiences available across the marketplace. What is more likely is that each of the established market segments will simply become smaller. There remain those who will pursue education in a campus setting and those who find the experience of online education to better fit their needs. Some will seek to combine formats. Students will be blessed with plentiful options and institutions will be cursed with a limited number of students, increasing costs, and strained resources.

Without a coordinated effort to undergird the higher education enterprise at the state, regional, or federal level, this enduring industry will absolutely survive, but it will change through an evolving pattern of assimilation. Each institution or system will make decisions deemed to be in its interest. It is not realistic to envision any meaningful, comprehensive intervention in this market sorting process. For such an effort to be impactful, it required development at least a decade ago, probably earlier. Accordingly, the task of the higher education community is to decide how these years ahead will unfold and whether there will again be a chance to think about the long-term future of higher education for American democracy.

Higher Education for American Democracy 2.0

In his letter of invitation to members of the President's Commission on Higher Education, US President Harry Truman began setting the context for the charge he was about to issue. Veterans from World War II were coming home and returning to college by the hundreds of thousands. Aware of this burden, he was eager to "assist the institutions to meet this challenge and to assure that all qualified veterans desirous of continuing their education have the opportunity to do so." The Serviceman's Readjustment Act of 1944, also known as the GI Bill, provided benefits, including support for education to returning service members. The broader opportunity envisioned for the nation was even more compelling. The letter went on to state:

It seems particularly important, therefore, that we should now reexamine our system of higher education in terms of its objectives, methods, and facilities; and in the light of the social role it has to play.

These matters are of such far-reaching national importance that I have decided to appoint a Presidential Commission on Higher Education. This Commission will be composed of outstanding civic and educational leaders and will be charged with an examination of the functions of higher education in our democracy and of the means by which they can best be performed. . . .

Among the more specific questions with which I hope the Commission will concern itself are: ways and means of expanding educational opportunities for all able young people; the adequacy of curricula, particularly in the fields of international affairs and social understanding; the desirability of establishing a series of intermediate technical institutes; the financial structure of higher education with particular attention for the rapid expansion of physical facilities. These topics of inquiry are merely suggestive and not intended to in any way limit the scope of the Commission's work. (Truman 1947)

The compelling call to action expressed in Truman's letter went beyond the matter at hand (i.e., returning veterans). The tyranny of the urgent would have stopped there, declaring the GI Bill enough for the federal government to tackle. If Truman had done so, he would have been saying to the system of higher education, "You figure it out." In one sense that is what happened because no comprehensive legislative package ever emerged. In fact, the letter made clear, "I am confident that the combined efforts of the educational institutions, the States, and the Federal Government will succeed in solving these immediate problems." It was from the outset the formulation of an agenda for every related entity to pursue on behalf of the nation. To be sure, there were all the practical realities to consider of organizational structures, personnel, facilities, and finance. The commission addressed all these concerns. The reason for undertaking the further development of a system was more than bricks and mortar, money, and hiring. It had to do with a commitment to democracy. The commission strongly asserted the national imperative for expanding equal access and opportunity for all. It argued for an education to promote the values of citizenship, international understanding, and cultural awareness. It viewed higher education as a means for reinforcing the social fabric of the nation and its people. This vision energized the work of many across the country to meet the challenges set before the nation.

More than 40 years into my career, I advocate for this level of thinking to be reignited. A renewal of an ambition to think comprehensively and plan incrementally through time changes the perspective of many and reshapes decision-making at all levels of higher education. The skeptic in me points to a current political landscape that has not been able to simply reauthorize the Higher Education Act since 2008. Our government is ill-prepared and ill-equipped to advance a far more complicated and comprehensive project on the scale Truman initiated. It is a sad and unfortunate reality.

Progress is still possible, however. The Truman Report was not without its controversies, so a perfect result was not necessary to animate the diffused authority and responsibility across the system. It was enough to have a broad consensus. One has to wonder, however, if a collective process in pursuit of a collective interest is still possible. If yes, I argue for a broad agenda to think about the future over decades, coupled with a time horizon that would make us feel like stonecutters building a cathedral. The work is undertaken with the knowledge that it is intended to benefit those who are not here yet, and those who are not born yet. As a national higher education enterprise, we have gone far too long without a sense of shared direction, and we are now paying the price as markets alone rule the day. Markets always have played a role, but it is now outsized and overtaking the national interest.

If the task is to be undertaken, it falls to leaders in the postsecondary universe willing to step forward and see it done within their realms of influence and advance the conversation wherever possible.

Accordingly, I conclude with words of advice for the many colleges and universities, state postsecondary systems, regional and professional accreditors, and institutional, academic, and professional associations that together provide opportunities to engage in honest discussions about the future. If in the end the markets are left to rule, then so be it. Many will still remain devoted to the task of teaching and learning and be of great service to the citizens of this county. The enterprise as a whole, however, will be reshaped by political winds, market pressures, and fiscal realities.

To the extent it is possible to promote a shared agenda, I offer the following advice:

1. Acknowledge the foundational aspects of higher learning that are enduring. Learning will remain a fundamentally human enterprise aided by various modalities of

instruction, facilitated by proper pedagogical design, and supported by appropriate technologies. The journey of education through a lifetime is the gradual transition of a dependent learner to an independent learner. Effective learning always involves human relationships.

2. Remember formal learning—in classrooms, laboratories, studios, and online programs—is extended and animated by informal learning through cocurricular, extracurricular, and work-based experiences. Learning that cooperates with well-defined patterns of human development is the most timely and impactful for the learner. It involves adaptation to the individual, acknowledging that one size does not fit all.

3. Realize that everything belongs to learning. The fullness of life experience applied to education is enriching. Involvement in student organizations and activities, competition and teamwork in athletics, shared artistic expression, and participation in communities of practice all enhance learning. Reducing this too far will result in one-dimensional thinking lacking in creative energy.

4. Remain committed to fostering learning as a function of citizenship. Education for the public good remains an important ideal. Democracy rests on the engagement of citizens to participate in all aspects of society. Society is also served well when personal fulfillment and civic engagement go hand in hand with vocational and professional pursuits. Education and democracy are inseparable.

5. Build a culture of inclusion and belonging that extends across the depth and breadth of diversity in all its forms. Facilitate the tensions, and sponsor dialogue and de-

bate. Ensure all voices are represented by creating access and opportunity for all to participate in and benefit from a rich learning experience.

6. Anticipate that education and workforce may become more loosely coupled in the years to come. Students will be ill-advised to "major in a job title" as career journeys become less defined and less predictable. The intent should be to prepare for the future by amassing all the knowledge, skill, and experience possible to open pathways to many different possibilities.

7. Beware of the risk of division by political ideology. Political migration is increasing in America as regions of this nation become increasingly identified with specific political perspectives. Press for independence of thought and free speech for all. Aim for education to generate light and not heat.

8. Explore emerging changes in lifestyle as the benefits and risks of residential campuses and online communities are weighed in the marketplace. More demand for personal accommodation is likely in the years to come with expectations for flexibility and customization. How students choose to live, work, and pursue education may change through time.

9. See the unfolding changes in intercollegiate athletics as a warning about the risks of commercialization and a drift away from mission—driven by money. As the definition of "student" morphs to accommodate the potential concurrent roles of athlete, musician, employee, business owner, or even vendor, bear in mind the potential conflicts of interest and commitment that may emerge

as students pay an institution for educational services and are also compensated for services they render through these collateral roles.

10. Accept that the future of higher education will be more about contraction than expansion as population demographics call for fewer and smaller institutions of higher education in the national enterprise. The market for postsecondary education will reshape the institutional and organizational landscape in higher education. The days ahead will be about rethinking the fundamental economics of higher education, not tinkering with a business model that will evolve on its own.

For all its inadequacies, the national enterprise for higher education is a marvel. It has demonstrated resilience far beyond that of other industries. Its enduring strength is found in its timeless qualities. Its features are amended slowly and carefully through assimilation. It responds to change processes that are incremental and respect the complexity of the enterprise when undertaken. It is seen and understood most clearly, not in a single moment, but through the long arc of time.

BIBLIOGRAPHY

AAUP (American Association of University Professors). 1940. *Statement of Principles on Academic Freedom and Tenure*. Washington, DC: AAUP. https://www.aaup.org/report/1940-statement-principles-academic -freedom-and-tenure.

AAUP (American Association of University Professors). 1966. *Statement on Government of Colleges and Universities*. Washington, DC: AAUP. https://www.aaup.org/report/statement-government-colleges-and -universities.

ACE (American Council on Education). 2023. *The American College President: 2023 Edition*. Washington, DC: ACE.

Birnbaum, Robert. 1988. *How Colleges Work: The Cybernetics of Academic Organization and Leadership*. San Francisco: Jossey-Bass.

Birnbaum, Robert. 1992. *How Academic Leadership Works: Understanding Success and Failure in the College Presidency*. San Francisco: Jossey-Bass.

Bolman, Lee G., and Terrence E. Deal. 1984. *Modern Approaches to Understanding and Managing Organizations*. San Francisco: Jossey-Bass.

Bolman, Lee G., and Terrence E. Deal. 1997. *Reframing Organizations: Artistry, Choice, and Leadership*. 2nd ed. San Francisco: Jossey-Bass, John Wiley & Sons.

Brenan, Megan. 2023. "Americans' Confidence in Higher Education Down Sharply." July 11, 2023. Washington, DC: Gallup. https://news .gallup.com/poll/508352/americans-confidence-higher-education -down-sharply.aspx.

CBO (Congressional Budget Office). 2023. *The Demographic Outlook: 2023 to 2053*. Washington, DC: CBO. https://www.cbo.gov/publication /58612#:~:text=In%20CBO%27s%20projections%2C%20the%20U .S.,population%20growth%20beginning%20in%202042.

Central College Bulletin. 1974. "Dr. Weller Calls 1974–75 Decisive Year." Central College, Pella, Iowa, September 1974.

Central College Bylaws. Central College, Pella, Iowa. Amended, January 23, 2021.

Cohen, Michael D., and James G. March. 1974. *Leadership and Ambiguity*. Boston: Harvard Business School Press.

Commission on the Future of Higher Education. 2006. *A Test of Leadership: Charting the Future of Higher Education*. Washington, DC: US Department of Education. http://www.ed.gov/about/bdscomm/list /hiedfuture/index.html.

Gallup. 2014. *Great Jobs Great Lives: The 2014 Gallup-Purdue Index Report*. Washington, DC: Gallup. https://www.gallup.com/services/176768 /2014-gallup-purdue-index-report.aspx.

Grawe, Nathan D. 2018. *Demographics and the Demand for Higher Education*. Baltimore, MD: Johns Hopkins University Press.

Iowa Code. 2023. Volume III. "Title VII Education and Cultural Affairs." Chapter 261I.2—Extracurricular Athletics, Approved March 3, 2022.

Keller, George. 1983. *Academic Strategy: The Management Revolution in American Higher Education*. Baltimore, MD: Johns Hopkins University Press.

Labaree, David F. 2017. *A Perfect Mess: The Unlikely Ascendancy of American Higher Education*. Chicago: University of Chicago Press.

Levine, Arthur, and Scott Van Pelt. 2021. *The Great Upheaval: Higher Education's Past, Present, and Uncertain Future*. Baltimore, MD: Johns Hopkins University Press.

Marken, Stephanie, and Zach Hrynowski. 2023. "Current College Students Say Their Degree Is Worth the Cost." June 1, 2023. Washington, DC: Gallup. https://news.gallup.com/poll/506384 /current-college-students-say-degree-worth-cost.aspx.

McCullough, David. 1977. *The Path between the Seas: The Creation of the Panama Canal 1870–1914*. New York: Simon & Schuster Paperbacks.

McGee, Jon. 2015. *Breakpoint: The Changing Marketplace for Higher Education*. Baltimore, MD: Johns Hopkins University Press.

Miller Center of Public Affairs, University of Virginia. "James A. Garfield." Accessed November 10, 2023. https://millercenter.org /president/garfield.

Morgan, Gareth. 1986. *Images of Organization*. Newbury Park, CA: Sage.

NCES (National Center for Education Statistics). n.d.a. *Digest of Education Statistics*. Washington, DC: US Department of Education. https:// nces.ed.gov/programs/digest.

NCES (National Center for Education Statistics). n.d.b. *Projections of Education Statistics to 2028*. Washington, DC: US Department of Education. https://nces.ed.gov/programs/pes.

NCES (National Center for Education Statistics). n.d.c. "Table 104.10: Rates of High School Completion and Bachelor's Degree Attainment among Persons Age 25 and Over, by Race/Ethnicity and Sex: Selected Years, 1910 through 2023." https://nces.ed.gov/programs /digest/d23/tables/dt23_104.10.asp?current=yes.

NCES (National Center for Education Statistics). n.d.d. "Table 302.20: Percentage of Recent High School Completers Enrolled in College, by Race/Ethnicity and Level of Institution: 1960–2022." https://nces .ed.gov/programs/digest/d23/tables/dt23_302.20.asp?current=yes.

O'Neill, Joseph P. 1983. "The Closing of a College: Resolving the Contradictions." *Change*, January/February 1983, 15, 22–27, 51.

O'Neill, Joseph P., and Samuel Barnett. 1980. *Colleges and Corporate Change: Merger, Bankruptcy, and Closing, A Sourcebook for Trustees and Administrators*. Princeton, NJ: Conference of Small Private Colleges.

Palmer, Parker J. 1983. *To Know as We Are Known: A Spirituality of Education*. New York: HarperCollins Publishers.

Parker, Kim. 2021. "What's Behind the Growing Gap between Men and Women in College Completion?" November 8, 2021. Washington, DC: Pew Research Center. https://www.pewresearch.org/short-reads /2021/11/08/whats-behind-the-growing-gap-between-men-and -women-in-college-completion.

President's Commission on Higher Education. 1947. *Higher Education for American Democracy*. 6 vols., New York: Harper & Brothers Publishers.

Putnam, Mark L. 1994. "The Role of Formal and Informal Sources of Information in Trustee Decision-Making at Small Private Colleges Struggling for Survival." EdD diss. Teachers College, Columbia University.

Putnam, Mark L. 2011. "Recovering from Failure." *Mark: My Words* (blog), *Central College*. March 3, 2011. https://president.central.edu/2011 /03/recovering-from-failure.

Putnam, Mark L. 2012. Education for Democracy: What's in It for Me?" *Mark: My Words* (blog), *Central College*. February 14, 2012. https:// president.central.edu/2012/02/education-for-democracy-whats-in -it-for-me.

Putnam, Mark L. 2022a. "Everything Belongs to Learning." *Civitas: A Journal of the Central College Community*, Central College. July 13, 2022. https://civitas.central.edu/2022/07/everything-belongs-to -learning.

Putnam, Mark L. 2022b. "Stewarding the Presidency," *Inside Higher Ed*, November 28, 2022. https://www.insidehighered.com/views/2022 /11/29/taking-long-view-presidency-opinion.

Putnam, Mark L. 2023. "Managing the Presidency through the Arc of Time," *Trusteeship* (January–February): 22–29.

Rudolph, Frederick. 1962. *The American College and University: A History*. New York: A. Knopf.

Schein, Edgar H. 1992. *Organizational Culture and Leadership*. 2nd ed. San Francisco: Jossey-Bass, John Wiley & Sons.

Simon, Herbert A. 1976. 3rd ed. *Administrative Behavior: A Study of Decision-Making Processes in Administrative Organization*. New York: The Free Press.

Taylor, Frederick W. 1911. *The Principles of Scientific Management*. New York: Harper and Brothers Publishers.

Thelin, John R. 2019. *A History of American Higher Education*. 3rd ed. Baltimore, MD: Johns Hopkins University Press.

Trachtenberg, Stephen Joel, Gerald B. Kauver, and E. Grady Bogue. 2013. *Presidencies Derailed: Why University Leaders Fail and How to Prevent It*. Baltimore, MD: Johns Hopkins University Press.

Truman, Harry S. 1947, July 13. "Letter Appointing Members to the National Commission on Higher Education." National Archive, Harry S. Truman Library and Museum. https://www.trumanlibrary .gov/library/public-papers/166/letter-appointing-members-national -commission-higher-education.

USCB (United States Census Bureau). 2020. *Quick Facts: Endicott Village, NY*. Washington, DC: USCB. https://www.census.gov/quickfacts/fact /table/endicottvillagenewyork/PST040223#PST040223.

Veysey, Laurence R. 1965. *The Emergence of the American University*. Chicago: University of Chicago Press.

Weber, Maximillian K. E. 1947. *The Theory of Social and Economic Organization*. New York: The Free Press.

WICHE (Western Interstate Commission for Higher Education). 2020. *Knocking at the College Door: Projections of High School Graduates*. Boulder, CO: WICHE. https://www.wiche.edu/wp-content/uploads /2020/12/Knocking-pdf-for-website.pdf.

Zemsky, Robert, Susan Shaman, and Susan Campbell Baldridge. 2020. *The College Stress Test: Tracking Institutional Futures Across a Crowded Market*. Baltimore, MD: Johns Hopkins University Press.

INDEX

Aoun, Joseph, 93, 94–95
artifacts, 52
assimilation of change: and dissent,
41; and external entities, 185–86;
and governance, 136; as gradual,
x–xi, 4–5, 8–9, 13–14, 20, 201;
and innovation, x, 171; intergenerational scale of, 195, 201; and
market forces, 38–39, 176; and
organizational theory, 45, 65; and
presidency, 100; and Six-Pack of
Change approach, 87–88; and
technology, 11–13, 83; and
Truman Report, x–xi, 34, 41–42,
189, 202; ubiquity of, 43, 91, 210.
See also conformity; convention
Association of American Colleges
and Universities (AAC&U),
142–44
Association of Governing Boards of
Universities and Colleges (AGB),
121, 136–39
assumptions, 52–53
athletics, 178–83, 184, 215–16
authority: of board, 147–48; of
faculty, 143–44; hierarchies of, 50;
lack of overall authority in higher
education, 9, 23–24, 25–30, 39;
and leadership, 64; and power,
57–58; of president, 99, 149, 150,
153; and shared governance,
143–44, 147–48, 149, 150, 153;
signing authority, 147–48
auto industry, 203, 204

Baldridge, Susan Campbell, 123
banking industry, 37, 202, 204, 209
Baptist Education Society of Iowa,
27
Barnett, Samuel, 198
Basic Educational Opportunity
Grant (BEOG), 75
Baumol effect (cost disease), 76–77,
192
Birnbaum, Robert, 46, 102–4,
106–7, 108, 109–10

boards: as communities of trust,
114–16, 120–22, 132–34; culture
of, 121–22; and decision-making,
123–33; and faculty, 142;
onboarding and succession
planning, 132; in organizational
theory exercise, 46–48; patterns
of, 121; and presidency, 99, 101,
102, 106, 108, 111–12, 113; and
relationships, 115–16, 131; role
of, 91, 113, 115–16; and shared
governance, 138–39, 141–42, 143,
146–48, 151–52, 153; tenures of
members, 117, 118, 119, 120; and
time frame of initiatives, 98,
132–33; and trustee model at
Central College, 116–21. *See also*
governance
Bogue, E. Grady, 101
Bolman, Lee, 53, 112
Borg metaphor: described, 8–9; and
external entities, 185–86; and
governance, 136; and gradual
change, 13–14, 36, 171, 201; and
organizational theory, 45, 65–66.
See also assimilation of change
Branstad, Terry, 168
Brown v. Board of Education, 189
budgets, 193, 207
bureaucracy, 49, 50, 56, 140

cable television industry, 205
Cain, Kacia, 78–79
canal building metaphor: described,
14–18; and governance, 136; and
organizational theory, 45, 65–66;
and systemic change, 20, 36–37,
201; and understanding challenges, 16–17, 37, 100
cathedral metaphor: described, 5–7;
and external entities, 185–86; and
governance, 136; and gradual
change, 7, 13–14, 36, 171, 201,
213–16; and intergenerational
structures, 6, 65, 201, 213; and
leaders, 20; and organizational

theory, 44–45, 65–66; and presidents, 100; and unchangeability of foundations, 9–11

Cathedral of St. John the Divine, 5–6, 195

Central College: author as presidential candidate, 94, 95, 116–17; and COVID-19 pandemic, 85–86; founding of, 27; governance model, 116–21, 149; repeat of challenges at, 67–69; and technology as vector of change, 82

challenges, understanding, 16–18, 37, 40, 201–2

change: agenda for, 213–16; vs. commitment to organizational structures, 54–55; and perception of resistance, 39, 200–201; pressure for quick, ix–x, 6–7, 18–19, 65–66; pressure to change higher education model, xi, 6–7, 8–9, 23–25, 170–71, 185, 194; scholarly interest in, 40–41. See also assimilation of change; Borg metaphor; canal building metaphor; cathedral metaphor; Six-Pack of Change approach

character traits and presidency, 102, 104, 105

charisma, 102, 103, 105

citizenship: and change agenda suggestions, 214; and education, 11, 33, 41–43, 164–68, 175–76, 213, 214; and norms, 84; and STEM, 78; and Truman Report, 41, 43, 163, 187, 212; and workforce, 80, 191. See also democracy

Civil Rights Act of 1964, 189

closings: author's dissertation on, 123–31, 196, 198; boards facing, 123–31; and demographics, 197; and enrollments, 197, 198–99; and finances, 197–200, 207; information and decision-making in, 123–31; and mattering,

197–98; reasons for, 197–200; threats of as cyclical/recurring, 67, 69, 70

Cohen, Michael, 55–64, 100, 112

Colleges and Corporate Change (O'Neill), 198–99

College Stress Test (Zemsky et al.), The, 123

Commission on Higher Education. See Truman Report

Commission on the Future of Higher Education. See Spellings Commission

Committee on Education Beyond the High School, 34

communication: and presidency, 107–8, 109, 150; and shared governance, 138, 139, 141, 145, 150, 151–52

community: boards as communities of trust, 114–16, 120–22, 132–34; partisanship and loss of, 114, 115

community colleges, 33

competition: and early development of colleges, 27, 28; global competitiveness, 22, 32; and market forces, 27, 29, 37–39, 42; for students, 194, 206–8

completion rates, 80

confidence: in higher education, 74; limits of to effect change, 17; and presidency, 103, 107

conformity: and administrators, 38; and boards, 121; and control, 155; and copying, 19; and evolution of higher education, 27–30, 36; and external entities, 184; and gradual change, x, xi, 5, 8–9, 14, 44, 91, 100, 132, 171, 176, 201; and market forces, 38, 176; and norms, 85; and organizational theory, 45, 65; and presidency, 100; and Six-Pack of Change approach, 87–88; and technology, 83

Congressional Budget Office (CBO), 72–73

Connecticut College, 93, 95
Consortium on Financing Higher
  Education (COFHE), 196–97
consumers, students as, 158, 206–8
contracts, 147–48
control: illusion of, 155; of students'
  learning, 158, 166, 172, 176
convention: and boards, 121; and
  conformity, 19; and evolution of
  higher education, 27–30; and
  external entities, 184; and gradual
  change, x, 5, 9, 44–45, 91, 132,
  171, 177, 201; and market forces,
  38, 176; and norms, 85, 115
Cook, Charles, 83–84
cooperation, 172–77
cost disease, 76–77, 192
costs: and business model, 207,
  208; and closings, 197–200; cost
  disease, 76–77, 192; and foundational beliefs of higher education,
  11–13; increases in, 37, 198;
  policymakers' focus on, 11–13;
  and quality of education, 67–68,
  76–77; and Spellings Commission,
  22; and technology, 81–82
costs and tuition, student: and
  economic uncertainty, 75–78, 80,
  87; and participation in higher
  education, 192–95; vs. prices,
  75–78, 192–93, 207
course design, 174–75
COVID-19 pandemic, 61–62, 85–86,
  88, 187
credentialing, 166, 169
credits and student costs, 193
culture war, 84–85

Deal, Terrence, 53, 112
debt: institutional, 133, 198–99;
  student, 187, 193
decision-making: and ambiguity,
  58–64, 125; and boards, 123–33;
  and COVID-19 pandemic, 61–62;
  and dissent, 63; and information,
  59, 61, 62, 123–31; and

organizational theory, 50–51,
  58–64; paralysis in, 127, 128, 130;
  and Six-Pack of Change approach,
  87–88; strategic planning
  example, 59–61; and transparency, 131; and trust, 124; on
  tuition pricing, 194
de Lesseps, Ferdinand, 15, 16, 17
democracy: and change agenda
  suggestions, 214; as focus in
  Truman Report, 31, 32, 41,
  163–65, 168, 211, 212; as
  foundational in education, 11,
  168, 210, 213. See also
  citizenship
Demographic Outlook, The (CBO),
  72–73
demographics: and change agenda
  suggestions, 216; demographic
  decline as change vector, 70–75,
  87; and enrollments, 73–75, 80,
  197, 206; and fertility rates,
  72–73; higher education's
  dependence on, 69, 70–75, 87,
  122–23, 128, 129, 188, 192, 197,
  206, 216; and industries in
  distress, 203; and policymakers,
  72–73; of presidents, 96; and
  Truman Report, 32
Department of Education: policy
  programs and initiatives, 22–25;
  and transgender athletes, 181,
  182
Dhawan, Tej, 119
Digest of Education Statistics, 73
dissent, 31, 33, 41, 63
distressed industries, 37–38, 203–6
diversity and inclusion in change
  agenda suggestions, 213–14
dual credit enrollments, 174, 193
Dutch Reformed Church, 27
duty of care, 141, 144

economics: and demographic decline,
  70–75; economic boosters and
  origins of higher education,

26–27; economic uncertainty as change vector, 70, 75–78, 87; and enrollments, 75, 80; and industries in distress, 203
education: and early learning, 10, 172; as human enterprise, 10. *See also* higher education; learning; lifelong learning; vocational education
Eisenhower, Dwight D., 34
Emergence of the American University, The (Veysey), 29, 30
emotions: and paralysis in decision-making, 127, 128; and professional distance, 102, 103–4, 105
Endicott-Johnson Shoes, 72
endowments, 13, 133, 193, 207
energy, 62, 63, 98, 100
enrollments: barriers to, 170; and budgets, 193; and closings, 197, 198–99; and COVID-19 pandemic, 187; current numbers, 36, 187; and decision to attend a school, 157–59; and demographics, 73–75, 80, 197, 206; dual credit, 174, 193; and economic uncertainty, 75, 80; and international students, 70; and market forces, 191–92; peak in, 205; and student costs, 170, 193; swings in, 88; and Truman Report, 32, 188
ethics, 101, 163, 176
exemplary presidency, 106, 108, 109–10, 112
experience, ambiguity of, 58
experiential learning, 162
external forces: numbers and types of, 183–84; and transgender athletes, 178–83. *See also* market forces

faculty: and boards, 142; and cost disease, 76; number of current, 36; in organizational theory exercise, 46–48; and presidency, 106, 107–8, 109, 111–12;

relationships as core to learning, 160–63; role of, 91; and tenure, 133, 141, 142–46; unionized, 145
faculty governance: at Central College, 116–20; and officers, 143–44; and presidency, 109, 150, 153; and shared governance, 138–46, 147, 150, 151, 153
failed presidency, 106, 108, 110, 112
farming industry, 203, 204
fertility rates, 72–73
financial aid: and economic uncertainty, 75; and participation in higher education, 170, 187, 188; as public policy success, 86; and sticker prices *vs.* net prices, 77–78, 192–93; and Truman Report, 33; and workforce preparation, 169
framing and reframing, 53, 112
Franks, Robert, 119
Freeland, Richard, 54, 93, 95
Freiberger, Chevy, 78
funding: decrease in state and federal, 193, 198, 208; and federal policy, 33, 35, 212; and Truman Report, 33
Future Ready Iowa, 79, 168–70

Gallup, 161–62
garbage cans, 59, 60, 62, 63–64
Garfield, James, 160
Gaudiani, Claire, 93, 95
gender: and completion rates, 80; transgender athletes, 178–83
GI Bill, 30, 86, 210–11
global competitiveness, 22, 32
governance: and community, 114–15; and innovation, 135–36; joint statement on, 137–39, 141, 145–47, 150, 151–52; *vs.* management, 152–53; and pressure for quick action, 18; role of, 135–36; using existing structures of, 152. *See also* boards

governance, shared: and administrators, 118, 138, 139, 147, 151, 153–54; and ambiguity, 144, 151–54; and authority, 143–44, 147–48, 149, 150, 153; boards, 138–39, 141–42, 143, 146–48, 151–52, 153; at Central College, 116–21, 149; and communication, 138, 139, 141, 145, 150, 151–52; and faculty, 109, 116–20, 138–46, 147, 150, 151, 153; and presidency, 109, 110, 138–39, 141–42, 143, 147, 149–51, 153; principles of, 137–39; and responsibilities, 139–40, 141, 143–46, 147, 149–51; students, 116–20, 138, 147, 158; and trust, 146

Grawe, Nathan D., 73–74

Great Jobs Great Lives (Gallup report), 161–62

Great Upheaval, The (Levine and Van Pelt), 40–41

Guiteau, Charles, 160

Hanson, Katharine, 196–97, 200

health care industry, 203, 204, 205

higher education: business model as failure, 207, 208; change agenda suggestions, 213–16; confidence in, 74; crises and adaptation, 89–90; crises as cyclical, 67–69; debates over participation in, 186–92; debates over purpose of, 163–67, 176; desirability of, 74, 80, 187–90; as distressed industry, 203–6; European model, 28; founding principles, 10–11; lack of overall design or authority, 9, 23–24, 25–30, 39; number of institutions, 36; origins of system, 25–30; percentage of Americans with baccalaureate degrees, 186; pressure to change higher education model, xi, 6–7, 8–9, 23–25, 170–71, 185, 194; as public good, 11, 163, 164–65;

quality of, 27, 67–68, 76–77; understanding history of before changing, xii, 36–43. *See also* assimilation of change; boards; Borg metaphor; canal building metaphor; cathedral metaphor; external forces; faculty; governance; learning; presidents; Six-Pack of Change approach

Higher Education Act of 1965, 35, 212

Higher Education for American Democracy. See Truman Report

history: lessons of, 195; need to understand, xii, 36–43; and role of leadership, 64

History of American Higher Education, A (Thelin), 33–34

Hopkins, Mark, 160

How Academic Leadership Works (Birnbaum), 102

How Colleges Work (Birnbaum), 46, 102

I Have a Plan program, 173

Images of Organization (Morgan), 51

immigration, 32, 73

independent learners, 10, 173

individual development and purpose of higher education, 163–67

inertia: and boards facing existential threats, 130; and COVID-19 pandemic, 88; and decision-making, 50, 59, 61–62; and presidency, 100–101; and salience, 60; and Six-Pack of Change approach, 88

inflation, 77, 88, 192

information: credibility of, 126–27; and decision-making, 59, 61, 62, 123–31; disinformation and falsified, 129, 130; informal, 124, 125, 128–29; as limited, 59; and organizational change, 54; validation of, 124, 125, 126

market forces: and assimilation, 38–39, 176; and change agenda suggestions, 216; and conformity and convention, 38, 176; and early college development, 12, 27–28, 29; and future of higher education, 202–3, 209–10, 213, 215, 216; and industries in distress, 37–38, 204–5; and participation in higher education, 191–92; and students as consumers, 158, 206–8; and tuition prices, 75–78, 192–95, 207

mattering, 197–98

McCullough, David, 15

means-end reversal, 24, 55, 162, 186

mentoring, 93–95, 162

mergers, 123, 208–9. *See also* closings

modal presidency, 106–8, 109, 110, 112–13

Modern Approaches to Understanding and Managing Organizations (Bolman and Deal), 53

Morgan, Gareth, 51

Morgan, Greta, 173

Morrill Land Grant Acts, 28

NAIA, 180, 181

narratives, 64–65, 99, 115, 132

National Center for Education Statistics (NCES), 73

National Postsecondary Education Cooperative (NPEC), 22–23

NCAA, 180, 181

New England Association of Schools and Colleges/New England Commission of Higher Education, 83

Nixon, Richard M., 34–35

No Child Left Behind policy, 25

norms, 70, 83–87, 115, 203

Northeastern University, 54–55, 93, 94–95

Nyack College, 75

O'Neill, Joe, 198–200

online models, 209, 210, 215. *See also* technology

organizational culture, 51–53

Organizational Culture and Leadership (Schein), 52–53

organizational theory: and ambiguity, 45, 51, 52, 53, 56–64; applying, 64–66; change *vs.* commitment to organizational structures, 54–55; complexity of, 48, 51, 53; and decision-making, 50–51, 58–64; framing and reframing, 53, 112; and norms, 84; and organizational culture, 51–53; overview of scholarship in, 48–54; and presidency, 100, 102; stakeholders scenario exercise, 46–48

overload, 59, 61, 62

Palmer, Parker, 160–61

Panama Canal, 15–18, 37

participation in higher education: and affordability, 192–95; and business model of higher education, 207; debates over, 186–92; and dissent, 63; estimates by Truman Report, 187–88; and financial aid, 187, 188; and segregation, 189–90; in STEM, 79

Path between the Seas, The (McCullough), 15

Pell Grants, 75

Perfect Mess, A (Labaree), 25

policymakers and public policy: and assimilation of changes, 11–13; cost focus, 11–13; and demographics, 72–73; and funding, 33, 35, 212; future, anxiety about, 200; and industries in distress, 203; and Kennedy and Nixon administrations, 34–35; limits on ability to effect change, 35, 37, 172; public policy as change

Schein, Edgar, 52–53
scientific management, 49
search process, presidency, 101–2, 104, 105–6, 111
segregation, 34, 189–90
Serviceman's Readjustment Act. *See* GI Bill
Shaman, Susan, 123
Siebert, Donald, 75, 76, 78
Simon, Herbert, 49–51, 53
Six-Pack of Change approach: and demographic decline, 70–75, 87; and economic uncertainty, 70, 75–78, 87; and industries in distress, 203; integrating, 87–90; interactions between vectors, 87, 88; and norms, 70, 83–85, 87; overview of, 70–71; and public policy, 70, 85–87; and technology innovation, 70, 81–83, 87; and workforce expectations, 70, 71, 72, 78–81, 87, 88
soft skills, 176–77
Spellings, Margaret, 21, 23, 25
Spellings Commission, 21–25, 35
sports. *See* athletics
stakeholders: and ambiguity of purpose, ix, 57; and organizational change goals, 55; and organizational theory exercise, 46–48; students as internal, 157–58
standards, 7, 174
Statement on Government of Colleges and Universities (joint statement), 137, 141, 145, 146–48, 150, 151–52
State Postsecondary Review Entities (SPREs), 24–25
status, 63, 80, 191
Steinke, Gary, 178
STEM, 78–79
"Stewarding the Presidency" (Putnam), 96
stewardship: and change over time, 6, 41; and presidency, 99, 103,

110–13, 150, 153; and shared governance, 138, 141, 150, 152, 153–54
strategic management, 69–70
strategic planning: decision-making example, 59–61; technology focus, 81–82
students: attrition rates, 187; choice in learning, 167–71; commercialization of athletes, 215–16; as consumers, 158, 206–8; decision to attend a school, 157, 159; as internal stakeholders, 157–58; international, 70; in organizational theory exercise, 46–48; preparedness of, 174–75; relationship to faculty, 160–63; relationship to institution, 158, 206; retention, 158, 206–7; and shared governance, 116–20, 138, 147, 158; soft skills, 176–77; transgender athletes, 178–83. *See also* costs and tuition, student; enrollments
Students for Fair Admissions (SFFA) v. Harvard, 190
Students for Fair Admissions (SFFA) v. University of North Carolina, 190
success: ambiguity in measures of, ix, 58; antecedents and planning, 17–18
Suez Canal, 15, 16, 17, 37
symbols: and ambiguity, 57, 58, 91; and culture war, 84–85; and norms, 84–85, 87; and organizational theory, 52, 57, 58, 59, 63, 64, 112, 135; and presidency, 99; visions as symbolic, 102–3

Taylor, Fredrick, 49
teachers: family as first, 172; role in learning, 10. *See also* faculty; faculty governance
technology: assimilation of, 11–13, 83; and costs, 81–82; and

COVID-19 pandemic, 88; and industries in distress, 203; innovation as change vector, 70, 81–83, 87; lack of overall design or authority for, 83; and marketplace, 209, 210; and strategic planning, 81–82
tenure, 133, 141, 142–46
helin, John R., 33–34
Thomas, Lia, 179
time: arc of time as asset, 14, 19–20, 216; and decision-making, 132–33; and energy, 62; needed for initiatives, 3–4, 17–18, 95–96, 98, 132–33; presidency as intergenerational, 99–101, 110–11, 113
Title IX, 181, 182
To Know as We Are Known (Palmer), 160–61
Trachtenberg, Stephen Joel, 101, 108
transfer credits, 193
transgender athletes, 178–83
transparency, 22, 101, 131
Truman, Harry S., x, 30, 210–12
Truman Report: assimilation and influence of, x–xi, 34, 41–42, 189, 202; and debate over purpose of higher education, 163–67, 176; and demand for higher education, 187–89; and democracy, 31, 32, 41, 163–65, 168, 211, 212; findings overview, 30–35; as model for change, 43, 201–2, 210–12; and segregation, 34, 189–90; and vocational education, 33, 165–66

trust: boards as communities of trust, 114–16, 120–22, 132–34; and decision-making, 124; and governance, 146; and likability, 103, 116; and norms, 115; and presidents, 103
trustees. *See* boards
tuition. *See* costs and tuition, student
Tuition Assistance Program (TAP Grant), 75

values, 52, 164
Van Kley, Eric, 157
Van Pelt, Scott, 40–41, 89
Veysey, Laurence, 29, 30
vision, 102–3, 105
vocational education, 33, 165–66

Weber, Max, 49
Weller, Ken, 68, 71
Wesselink, Dave, 119
Western Interstate Commission on Higher Education (WICHE), 73
workforce: and change agenda suggestions, 215; and debates over participation, 191; expectations as change vector, 70, 71, 72, 78–81, 87, 88; and financial aid, 169; and industries in distress, 203; policymakers focus on, 78–80, 87, 164, 166–70, 176; and Truman Report, 21, 32; workplace engagement, 161–62

Zemsky, Robert, 123
Zook, George F., 31

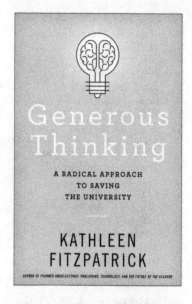

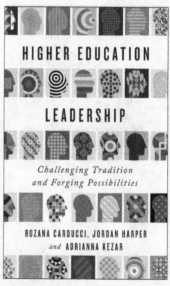